Write *THE* *Vision*

Christian Mission and Modern Culture

EDITED BY
ALAN NEELY, H. WAYNE PIPKIN,
AND WILBERT R. SHENK

In the series:

Believing in the Future, by David J. Bosch

Write the Vision, by Wilbert R. Shenk

Write THE *Vision*

The Church Renewed

———

WILBERT R. SHENK

TRINITY PRESS INTERNATIONAL
Valley Forge, Pennsylvania

Gracewing

First U.S. edition
published 1995 by
TRINITY PRESS INTERNATIONAL
P.O. Box 851
Valley Forge, PA 19482-0851
U.S.A.

First British edition
published 1995 by
GRACEWING
2 Southern Avenue
Leominster
Herefordshire HR6 0QF
England

Scripture quotations are from the New Revised Standard Version
Bible, copyright 1989, Division of Christian Education of the Na-
tional Council of the Churches of Christ in the United States of
America, and are used by permission.

Cover design: Brian Preuss

Library of Congress Cataloging-in-Publication Data

Shenk, Wilbert R.
    Write the vision : the Church renewed / Wilbert R. Shenk.
       p.   cm. — (Christian mission and modern culture)
    Includes bibliographical references.
    ISBN 1-56338-118-4 (Trinity Press)
    ISBN 0-85244-334-X (Gracewing)
    1. Church renewal.   2. Missions—Theory.   3. Civilization,
Modern—20th century.   I. Title.   II. Series.
BV600.2.S524   1995
262'.001'7—dc20   95-16095
                                        CIP

Printed in the United States of America

95   96   97   98   99   00   6   5   4   3   2   1

Contents

90020

Preface to the Series

Both Christian mission and modern culture, widely regarded as antagonists, are in crisis. The emergence of the modern mission movement in the early nineteenth century cannot be understood apart from the rise of technocratic society. Now, at the end of the twentieth century, both modern culture and Christian mission face an uncertain future.

One of the developments integral to modernity was the way the role of religion in culture was redefined. Whereas religion had played an authoritative role in the culture of Christendom, modern culture was highly critical of religion and increasingly secular in its assumptions. A sustained effort was made to banish religion to the backwaters of modern culture.

The decade of the 1980s witnessed further momentous developments on the geopolitical front with the collapse of communism. In the aftermath of the breakup of the system of power blocs that dominated international relations for a generation, it is clear that religion has survived even if its institutionalization has undergone deep change and its future forms are unclear. Secularism continues to oppose religion, while technology has emerged as a major source of power and authority in modern culture. Both confront Christian faith with fundamental questions.

The purpose of this series is to probe these developments from a variety of angles with a view to helping the church understand its missional responsibility to a culture in crisis. One important resource is the church's experience of two centuries of cross-cultural mission that has reshaped the church into a global Christian *ecumene*. The focus of our inquiry will be the church in modern culture. The series (1) examines modern/postmodern culture from a missional point of view; (2) develops the theological agenda that the church in modern culture must address in order to recover its own integrity; and (3) tests fresh conceptualizations of the nature and mission of the church as it engages modern culture. In other words, these volumes are intended to be a forum where conventional assumptions can be challenged and alternative formulations explored.

This series is a project authorized by the Institute of Mennonite Studies, research agency of the Associated Mennonite Biblical Seminary, and supported by a generous grant from the Pew Charitable Trusts.

Editorial Committee

ALAN NEELY

H. WAYNE PIPKIN

WILBERT R. SHENK

Introduction

The relation of the gospel to culture ought to be a subject of permanent reflection and debate among Christians. But the church's preoccupations are many, and this concern has suffered frequent eclipse. With the rise of the modern missionary movement in the nineteenth century, exotic new questions were given priority — *inter alia,* polygamy, *sati,* other religions, and indigenization. In the twentieth century attention turned to the West and the relation between modern culture and the gospel where the historic heartland of Christianity appeared to be increasingly inhospitable to Christian faith and the great churches of Christendom adopted a defensive mode. William Temple declared, "Our problem is to envisage the task of the Church in a largely alien world." Temple was one leader who harbored few illusions about the real status and authority of the established church in modern culture.

Periodically, someone has set off an alarm, and the churches have responded with official initiatives such as the Church of England's Archbishops' Committee on Inquiry on the Evangelistic Work of the Church in 1918. As Archbishop of Canterbury, William Temple himself took the lead in establishing a Commission on Evangelism in 1943. He did not live to see the final, widely publicized report

Towards the Conversion of England (1945), which recommended a comprehensive mobilization of the whole church for a new evangelistic thrust. Adrian Hastings (1986:437) has judged this plan to have been "a very damp squib," a vacuous exercise.

Whether one examines reports produced by official church commissions or the rationales that govern parachurch evangelistic associations, one uncovers little to suggest that these initiatives have taken as their starting premise that the church in modern Western culture faces "a largely alien world" every bit as demanding as any culture encountered by the missionary during the heyday of the modern mission movement. Typically, these well-intentioned but prosaic pronouncements fail to engage the fact that the gospel itself is at odds with the plausibility structure and controlling worldview of modern culture. Any initiative that does not recognize this fact is bound to produce nothing more than a well-modulated echo of modern culture.

This volume presents a reconnaissance of the church-modern culture nexus in terms of its historical roots and development over the centuries. The thesis may be stated as follows: The engagement of the church with modern Western culture has resulted in the marginalization of Christian faith. During this same period the missionary movement has been the catalyst for extending the faith to other continents with the result that the majority of Christian adherents are now to be found outside the West. This underscores the importance of mission for ecclesial identity and vitality. The European church had been under siege already before the modern period, with the integrity of the church of Christendom fundamentally compromised by its alliance with political and military power. A corollary of this lack of integrity was the way the church of Christendom suppressed mission to its own culture. Because it developed in the shadow of historical Christendom, evangelization in modern culture offers a significant case study of how mission to culture is foreclosed when the means and methods are controlled by culture. The story of the people of God moves between two poles: apostasy and renewal, failure to live by their covenant responsibility alternating with a reawakening to the vocation for which God's people exist. The legacy of Christendom has hobbled the church in responding to the vigorous challenge of modern culture to faith. The rapid erosion of the old structures of Christendom over the past three centuries may be a necessary — but nonetheless painful — stage in rehabilitating the church. One thing appears certain: when the church in the West is truly renewed, it will be a church with integrity and a clear sense of its mission to its own culture. These two elements are indivisible.

A caveat to the reader is in order. In such brief compass, one cannot present a carefully nuanced and finely balanced treatment. The goal is to sketch out a proposition that can continue to be debated and tested. Two terms figure prominently in the discussion here: Christendom and the Enlightenment. Some readers may feel these historical developments have been treated too unappreciatively. By any reckoning, historical Christendom and the Enlightenment have been two of the defining developments in history, especially with respect to the church. Our purpose is to understand the main historical and sociological influences with which we must come to terms in a time of cultural crisis and transition. Both Christendom and the Enlightenment have had an incalculable shaping influence on the church in modern Western culture. It is incumbent on us to acknowledge with gratitude the positive contributions of this legacy while critically examining those dimensions that do not advance the reign of God and from which the church must be freed if it is to be renewed.

The main ideas that inform this volume have been developed in various lectures over the past several years. The present outline took shape when I had the privilege to give the annual Mission of the Church Lectures at Emmanuel School of Religion, Johnson City, Tennessee, November 3–5, 1993, on the theme "Why Mission to Western Culture?" Portions of Chapter 1 were included in a presentation to the second annual Gospel and Our Culture Network Consultation, held in Chicago, Illinois, February 18–20, 1993, and subsequently published in the *International Bulletin of Missionary Research* 18 (January 1994): 1. Chapter 2 overlaps in one section with my essay in *The Good News of the Kingdom — Mission Theology for the Third Millennium*, edited by Charles Van Engen, Dean S. Gilliland, and Paul Pierson (Maryknoll, N.Y.: Orbis Books, 1993). I am grateful to Dean C. Robert Wetzel and his colleagues at Emmanuel for listening constructively and critically and receiving me so cordially. Leslie P. Fairfield and Taylor Burton-Edwards helped me by their careful reading of the first draft of the manuscript. David Lowes Watson and Darrell L. Guder kindly read the penultimate draft and offered further suggestions. Finally, I acknowledge with gratitude the moral support and encouragement of Dean Gayle Gerber Koontz and the award of a research unit by the Associated Mennonite Biblical Seminary the fall of 1993 in order to complete this manuscript.

1

Integrity

One of the most disturbing observations that confronts the church in modern Western culture is that both Roman Catholic and Reformation churches have been in a long phase of decreasing adherents and increasing cultural marginality. This fact has weighed on thoughtful church leaders for more than a hundred years, but concern has intensified as the twentieth century has progressed. Numerous studies have sought to explain this trend in terms of the historical-cultural environment — especially the Enlightenment, the rise and triumph of science, and the consequent secularization of modern culture.

This is not to posit church membership and social position as the primary indicators of the church's health. Rather, these are symptoms that point to an etiology to be found within the church itself. Two clues that suggest that the search might fruitfully start with a probe of ecclesial reality are the relation of the church to freedom of religion and the growth of the church beyond the bounds of historical Christendom.

The liberal vision of modern society formulated in the eighteenth century included freedom for individuals to believe and practice the religion, or no religion, of their choice according to the dictates of conscience. Many Europeans who immigrated to North America during the seventeenth to nineteenth centuries, for example, were driven by the desire to escape the illiberal constraints of the established church or government in order to practice religion in freedom. The democratic vision of human rights, including the freedom to believe and practice the faith of one's choice, spread, and persecution based on religious convictions largely disappeared from the West. But after more than two centuries, can we demonstrate that religious freedom has translated into spiritual vitality for the church in modern Western culture? In fact, contemporary instances of significant ecclesial vitality are not to be found in societies that have democratic governments. For examples of vigorous Christian witness in the twentieth century we invariably turn to churches in situations of overt oppression. We must concede that political freedom is not a correlate of spiritual vigor.

The second clue comes from the modern missionary movement, which has contributed to the unprecedented extension of the Christian faith worldwide during the past two centuries. Concurrent with the decline of the church of Christendom in the West, the church has taken root and grown in Asia, Africa, and Latin America to such an extent that the majority of Christian adherents today are to be found outside the West. In the missionary situation, the issue of gospel and culture cannot be avoided, nor can it be settled on terms set by culture. Whenever the church relates to its context in self-consciously missional terms, it responds in a fundamentally different mode than when it views itself as chaplain to society.

The credibility of the church in modern culture continues to be at issue. We will argue from history that a lack of integrity has undermined the credibility of the church in modern Western culture. Whenever the church is controlled by culture, it forfeits its prophetic word. To have credibility and command the loyalty of its members, the church must have ecclesial integrity. The notion of "integrity" carries a twofold meaning. On the one hand, a person who lacks integrity is dishonest. On the other, a lack of integrity indicates incompleteness. Both dimensions are at issue in the historical examples we will consider.

The Character of the Church

It is a portent of our times that some of the most acute analyses of what the church is and ought to be are coming from Asia, Africa, and Latin America. Liberation theology has made a particularly important contribution to the Christian *ecumene* in this regard.

José Míguez Bonino (1975:155), a liberation theologian, has argued that "the ecclesiological question is critical for all contemporary theology." He traces the problem back to the ecclesiologies of the Reformation and Counter-Reformation. These ecclesiologies, formulated to prove that the "other" was a "false" church, are now in crisis. Sixteenth-century ecclesiologies all assumed a Christendom context. "In a predominantly static, intellectualistic, and juridically minded frame of reference, the criteria adopted were backward-looking." They were cast in institutional terms to defend a historical tradition. These ecclesiologies have come to grief because of the accelerating dissolution of Christendom and the growing awareness of the historically conditioned nature of doctrine and church. Recent attempts to rethink the church from a biblical and theological basis have demonstrated that in scripture the church is interpreted largely in terms of its purpose in relation to the *missio Dei,* whereas classical Christendom ecclesiologies emphasized its institutional character. A contemporary counterexample, the Latin American Base Ecclesial Communities, suggests that a hierarchically and magisterially defined church holds little promise for the future. Only one that takes form in the faith of the people can have staying power (Boff 1986).

The church is indispensable for sustaining Christian faith. Yet the church must have a character that allows it to embrace peoples of the most diverse backgrounds, and must do so across time. When the church allows itself to be taken captive by a particular culture, ethnic group, or class, it forfeits its claim to be a faithful witness to the reign of God. This has crucial implications both for the individual Christian and for the church itself. For the individual who is seeking to be a faithful disciple, the reality of the church will either support or undercut discipleship. Loyalty to the church cannot be sustained over time if there is lack of congruence between the gospel and the existential ecclesial reality.

The problem is not a new one; indeed, it must be addressed in each generation. And we cannot confidently call the church to missional engagement with modern culture unless we face the critics and accusers who see the contemporary church as being deeply compromised. A lack of integrity discredits the church both in the eyes of its own members and the world. The recovery of integrity is an essential first step.

A Christian Culture?

People speak readily of "Christian" culture as though its meaning is self-evident. This is, at best, an ambiguous notion on both biblical and historical grounds. The New Testament gives us no basis for thinking in these terms. There the emerging messianic community, seeking to be faithful to the reign of God revealed in Jesus the Messiah, continually encounters the other kingdom that is opposed to God's will. The whole of the New Testament is shaped by this reality. The faithful community is given no license to believe that its future will be secured by any power other than that demonstrated by God in the crucified and resurrected Messiah.

On this point there is continuity between Old and New Testaments, a point that emphasizes the importance of a *canonical* approach to this theme. For already in the Old Testament the reader has been amply warned against putting confidence in any religio-cultural synthesis based on political power as a way of ensuring fidelity to God. On the contrary, the prophets preached about an unconventional order that contrasted sharply with the cultural status quo by inverting all human expectations through a reordering of life in conformity to God's will (Jeremiah 31:31–33). The people of God were called to join this new order of which God was the leader.

To be semantically and historically accurate, we should distinguish between "Christian culture" and "Christendom." The latter is the correct designation for the synthesis forged after 313 c.e. by Emperor Constantine and his successors. Christendom meant that Christianity became recognized as the religion of state, and the church functioned as the religious guardian of society. Christendom, or the *corpus Christianum,* thereby became indistinguishable from society. Citizenship in society was synonymous with membership in the church, and baptism was a religio-political rite. It is quite another matter to judge the extent to which this religio-cultural arrangement is demonstrably *Christian* and can be deemed a faithful instrument of the reign of God in the world.

In his widely read book *The Unfinished Task,* Stephen Neill (1957:98–102) took up the question of "Christian culture" as part of an agenda as yet unfinished. The crucial question is the set of criteria by which we measure the "Christliness" of a culture. It is instructive to note the cautions and qualifications Neill invokes. He first asserts that we can speak of a culture as Christian only when the gospel has penetrated into the personal and social subconscious of a people, so that it influences human behavior instinctively. To warn against an easy formulaic use of this dictum, Neill avers that such a synthesis between Christian faith and culture has happened but rarely. Only twice in the past two thousand years has such a union taken place at all. Neill describes these two instances briefly.

In the fifth century Augustine wrote his great work *The City of God,* which was to shape Christian thought for the next thousand years. Augustine's achievement came at the end of the process that culminated in this first synthesis, and it began to break apart almost immediately thereafter. In the fifteenth century the Italian poet Dante led in forging for the second time such a synthesis between Christianity and culture. Again, this achievement came at the end of a long buildup and was followed immediately by disintegration. With such fragile historical cases at hand, Neill does not advance his case with any self-confidence.

Then he turns to the question: How "Christian" was England, one of the leading powers in later Christendom? Neill argues that at most one can speak of a "near synthesis" in two brief periods. The first of these occurred during the second half of Elizabeth I's reign in the sixteenth century when there was a rapid diffusion of the Bible among the English people. A second near union happened during the Victorian Age when the impact of the Evangelical Revival was felt in many ways, including the spread of education among the masses so that most villages and towns had primary schools with the Bible as the basis of education. Church attendance was at a peak, and people were hearing the Bible read regularly. In both instances the Bible was the active agent in bringing Christian influence to bear on the wider culture.

The rapid decline of religious influence in English culture coincided with the rise of a new generation of writers and novelists — including H. G. Wells, Arnold Bennett, and John Galsworthy — who were either ignorant of the Bible and the Christian tradition or hostile to it. It is said that playwright and wit George Bernard Shaw learned just enough of the Christian faith to be able to take cheap shots at it.

In the 1980s it was observed that contemporary British high school students who understood Milton and Dante were not the descendants of the Anglo-Saxons but the sons and daughters of recent Muslim immigrants. For them religious language and symbols out of the monotheistic faith tradition continue to furnish meaning in the Muslim universe of discourse, whereas for old-line Anglo-

Saxons symbols drawn from modern culture have taken over.

A leitmotiv running through the modern period is the bankruptcy of Christendom as carrier of Christian reality. It shows up in studies of literature, history, theology, and sociology. How dare anyone claim that Western culture is *Christian?* The tension produced by the discrepancy between churchly reality and official creed has caused concerned people in every generation to press for renovation of the church so that it might live wholly under the lordship of Jesus Christ rather than in subservience to worldly power, and that the church might demonstrate in its own life a commitment to righteousness/justice. This dissent has come from two distinct sectors of the church.

Since the Protestant Reformation a tributary of dissent has established itself over against the ecclesiastical mainstream precisely at this point. Such dissenters, who had to make their critique from the periphery, typically were stigmatized as sectarians. That fact is well known and needs no further elaboration here. But there has been a second source of critique. This is represented by dissenting voices from within the established, or mainstream, churches, leaders who have decried the fundamental lack of integrity of the church and the consequences this holds for the church's relation to the world. These have been credentialed leaders and devout members of the church. As loyal adherents of the established church, their testimony could not readily be dismissed on grounds that they were sectarians. They believed that their very fealty required them to inveigh against the church's compromised character. What is remarkable is the strength of resistance the ecclesiastical hierarchy marshalled against these prophets. Instinctively the hierarchy erected an impermeable shield against reform initiatives. One of the most fascinating case studies in this regard comes from the early decades of the modern period and is concerned with John Wesley and the movement in which he was the dominant figure for some fifty years.

John Wesley and the Working Masses

On August 24, 1744, John Wesley preached before the University of Oxford. As a fellow of Lincoln College, on average he was called upon to preach every three years before the university. Wesley had a reputation for drawing larger-than-usual audiences. He took as his theme on this occasion "Scriptural Christianity." He had not come to tickle the ears of his auditors. Indeed, his intention was to confront a situation he considered intolerable.

In his sermon Wesley contrasted the lifestyle of university men with the life of true Christian piety as set forth in the Scriptures. He characterized university men — both faculty and students — as being guilty of gluttony, avarice, luxury, sensuality, drunkenness, and pride. It was of course patently bad taste, on Wesley's part, to comment on the behavior of fellow university men in such an unsparing manner.

As Wesley reached the climax of his argument, he posed several rhetorical questions: "Where does this [Scriptural] Christianity now exist? With what propriety can we term any a Christian country, which does not answer this description?" Wesley exhorted his audience: "Why then, let us confess we have never yet seen a Christian country upon earth" (Sugden 1921:1:104f). John Wesley had risked making a calculated attack.

Retribution came swiftly. The university vice-chancellor immediately sent for Wesley's sermon notes, a signal that his sermon was being officially reviewed. John Wesley had breached all etiquette. Never again would he preach before the university.

When Wesley was born in 1703 the nation was in crisis. Britain was still in the aftermath of the civil war. What remained of the feudal system, at the heart of which was the intertwining of church and state, was steadily crumbling. The Enlightenment dynamic was permeating all areas of human existence, unsettling established ways and encouraging people to pursue new ones. Eighteenth-century society was undergoing many changes, and the culture was in upheaval. The foundations of the industrial revolution were being laid, and as the century wore on, new industry began to emerge from which the privileged few would gain unprecedented prosperity while the masses would actually sink deeper into poverty.

James Woodforde's remarkable *The Diary of a Country Parson 1758–1802* depicts a society of egregious inequities firmly held in place by economic and class structures. During the winter of 1794–95 special distributions of bread were made to the poor of Woodforde's parish, but his diary records frequent sumptuous meals for the parson and his friends.[1] Little wonder the upper classes lived in constant fear of the "crowd" during the eighteenth century because of repeated rioting over food shortages (Thompson 1971: 76–136).

The Church of England's Convocation, the official assembly where affairs of church were dealt with, had long been suspended. The church was quite unprepared to respond to the changing situation with its pressing new pastoral needs. The hierarchy refused to adjust the out-dated ecclesiastical system to accommodate to the pastoral challenge of the thousands of people who were driven by economic necessity from their rural homes into the growing conurbations.

John Wesley deliberately directed his ministry to the masses beyond the pale of the church, fully conscious that the church had neither the will nor the imagination to go to the people. In this Wesley broke rank with his fellow evangelists. They found their audiences largely among the rising middle class and the lesser nobility who already were connected to the church (Outler 1991:27). Wesley's field of labor was among the masses who did not see the church as their ally. No other movement in the eighteenth century reached the working class as did Wesley's.

Wesley incorporated other notable features in his strategy for breaking free from the traditional ecclesiastical system in order to reach the masses who were alienated from the Christian faith. He insisted on a plain, direct style of communication in order to be fully accessible to ordinary people (Webb 1988:202–11). In contrast to the church which refused to make structural adaptations, he organized new believers into cell groups or class meetings to provide spiritual nurture and social support.

Wesley quickly became an advocate for the working class, writing many letters to newspapers commenting on oppressive social and economic injustices. In 1772 he wrote a letter that appeared in several newspapers on the causes of unemployment and rising prices: "Why are pork and poultry and eggs so dear? Because of the monopolizing of farms, as mischievous a monopoly as was ever introduced into these kingdoms. The land which was formerly divided among ten or twenty little farms enabled them comfortably to provide for their families but is now generally engrossed by one great farm.... How can the price of wheat be reduced? By prohibiting for ever that bane of health, that destroyer of strength, of life, and of virtue, *distilling*" [*sic*] (:6). Because of Wesley's peripatetic way of life, he was undoubtedly one of the best-informed observers of life in the British Isles in his day. His words carried authority.

If we compare the lifework of Wesley and George Whitefield, important contrasts emerge. They differed theologically in their understanding of grace, and this led them to different positions concerning discipleship and pastoral care. They also differed on churchmanship. In contrast to Wesley, Whitefield chose not to contest the ecclesiastical structures, with the result that his influence was confined largely to the church. Wesley reached thousands for whom the established church was not an option by effectively constructing alternative communities of spiritual and social welfare.

Søren Kierkegaard's "Attack on Christendom"

Few can match Kierkegaard's impassioned critique of Christendom, especially in his writings from the last two years of his life, 1854–55 (1968). Like Wesley, Kierkegaard was thoroughly offended by the hypocrisy of the hierarchy of the Danish State Church, the mechanical routine of church religion, and the subservience of the church to culture. He decried "this prodigious castle in the air: Christian states, kingdoms, lands; this playing with millions of Christians who reciprocally recognize one another in their mediocrity, yet are all of them believers.... Christianity simply does not exist.... The sort of men who now live cannot stand anything so strong as the Christianity of the New Testament." Kierkegaard insisted that "Christendom" rested on two lies: it domesticated Christianity to worldliness and then interpreted the absence of all persecution of the faith as progress. "The fact is," he said, "that there is nothing to persecute" (:277, 279).

Kierkegaard opposed philosophical systems, such as Hegel's, based on idealism rather than living experience. Intellectualist approaches to Christian faith showed little interest in the realities of the church and ordinary people. Kierkegaard countered this with a strong emphasis on personal responsibility and commitment as the route to authentic discipleship, two themes noticeably absent from contemporary mainstream theology. He put a premium on personal decision.

Kierkegaard's perduring legacy is that of a powerful but solitary voice that focused the spotlight on the state of the church of Christendom, in particular its observed lack of integrity. No organizer, the "brooding Dane" left little lasting impact on the church or on the understanding of the Christian life in his own time. In the twentieth century Kierkegaard's genius came to be appreciated.

A. F. Winnington-Ingram: A Failure of Vision

During Easter Term of 1895 Arthur Foley Winnington-Ingram (1896), head of Oxford House in East London, delivered six lectures on pastoral theology in the Divinity School, Cambridge University. Oxford House was the Anglo-Catholic Mission to East London, a work founded in 1856.

Winnington-Ingram, subsequently Bishop of London 1901–39, was not a profound thinker, but with a pastor's passion he described conditions in East London at the end of the nineteenth century. East London left the observer with the overwhelming impression of overcrowding. Housing was in such short supply that typically a worker, his wife, and several children had to make do with a single room. A four-room house would be occupied by four families who had to share cooking and toilet facilities (McIlhaney 1988). For the church this meant that parishes were too large to allow for adequate pastoral care. Besides the working class masses, other classes inhabited East London, and the sense of class divisions ran deep.

All of this had direct implications for the church. Winnington-Ingram was well aware that "mixed up with this class feeling — there is the *feeling against the church* [*sic*]. . . . [T]he Church is largely looked on still as the Church of the higher class, and as being always conservative" (:5). This left the church effectively marginalized from the masses. Winnington-Ingram reported that city dwellers were a "hotbed of all kinds of curious opinions," meaning secularism and unbelief. Often enough people embraced esoteric ideas as a way of acting out their antipathy for the church.

In Winnington-Ingram and his cohorts one meets deep empathy for the people of East London counterposed to their own ingrained pride of class. He argued that it was unreasonable to try to "convert" working class people to "Church ways," expecting such people who worked ten- to fourteen-hour days, six days a week, to turn out on Sunday morning to attend mass. And yet essentially he and his mission could not see beyond the status quo. They offered to East London the standard church program.

In making his appeal to Cambridge students to join the mission, Winnington-Ingram emphasized that this was a true frontier of "new country and treading fresh ground: It is not that the Church of God has lost the great towns; it has never had them" (:22). It seemed not to occur to Winnington-Ingram that the frontier lay as much within the church itself as with the masses of East London. In Winnington-Ingram one meets heroic compassion and pastoral concern; but, in contrast to John Wesley, he dared not touch the structures and patterns that separated the church from the masses.

Both Anglo-Catholic and Evangelical Anglicans sent missions to East London. An impressive outpouring of people and other resources continued for more than one hundred years. Those who have evaluated it judge it to have been a remarkable failure. This missionary effort failed precisely where Wesley had succeeded. It never effectively engaged and responded to the class barrier. The missions continued sending Oxford-educated "gentlemen" and "ladies" whose goal it was, like that of Professor Henry Higgins, to transform all the Eliza Doolittles of East London into proper English ladies and gentlemen (McIlhaney: chap. 5).

Emergence of the Working Class

The experience of this mission to East London must be situated within the wider sociohistorical frame of reference. The eighteenth and nineteenth centuries in Europe were tumultuous. Industrialization brought in its wake a bewildering range of adjustments as traditional culture was forcibly drawn into modern technological society. The living standards of various groups of workers were affected in contrasting ways. E. P. Thompson warns (1966:242) that it is a problem that "presents endless complexities." He observes that "the first half of the 19th century must be seen as a period of chronic underemployment, in which the skilled trades are like islands threatened on every side by technological innovation and by the inrush of unskilled or juvenile labour."[2] The groups that made up the laboring classes were in constant competition with one another, and this was only intensified by "the general *insecurity* of many skills in a period of rapid technical innovation and of weak trade union defences" (:243). Technological innovation, a core value of modern industrial society, constantly devalued the old and elevated the new. Against continual innovation there appeared to be no rational defense. The spectacle of the Luddites only seemed to confirm how right perpetual innovation was.

A European working class with its own identity was fully formed by the end of the nineteenth century (McLeod 1980:191–214; 1981). Religion played an uncertain role in working class life. In some areas religion was an important part of working class identity, but more typically the working class ethos was at odds with church, state, and employer. In other words, the working class ethos was a mechanism for coping with the powers of the larger society.

Although the city was the scene of overt "dechristianisation," we will be misled if we treat the process as a simple straightforward development when, in fact, it consisted of several strands. Multiple models are required if we are to understand the varieties of "dechristianisation." One model describes groups that were not Christian in their traditional villages and who remained outside the church after moving to the city. Another group consists of working class people who in the city were increasingly alienated from their traditional moorings in the church. Some of these people moved into the political left wing. There is a third model. The French revolution of 1789 directly encouraged working people to embrace democratic and egalitarian ideals. These ideals were more easily joined to humanist philosophy than to the traditional church. Secularism had particular appeal in this circumstance. In all three cases, the city provided little, if any, incentive to the working class to consider the church.

Under such conditions, where the "dechristianisation" process was an important force, the church remained largely unadapted to the urban milieu (Wasdell 1977). At the same time emerging political ideologies emphasized class differences and struggle. The church was largely unable to bridge class differences, further weakening the church's credibility in modern society.

As the nineteenth century ended and the twentieth began, a new sense of crisis marked Western culture. The German philosopher Friedrich Nietzsche gave a particularly gloomy prognosis and propounded the philosophy of nihilism.[3] World War I only intensified the disillusionment over the failure of the doctrine of unlimited evolutionary progress. Because the church of Christendom was so deeply implicated in modern culture, though, few loyalists saw any alternative except to stay aboard the sinking ship. It is the few visionaries, however, who are still worth paying attention to.

Walter Hobhouse's Call
for a Missionary Ecclesiology

One of the most remarkable treatises on church and world in the early twentieth century is that by Walter Hobhouse (1911), *The Church and the World in Idea and History,* delivered as the Bampton Lectures for 1909 in Oxford. Hobhouse left no doubt that he considered the present crisis in the church to be the direct result of the primordial compromise the church had entered into beginning "with the conversion of Constantine." Hobhouse offered an elaborate analysis of the historical outworking of this compromise and proposed that reform of the church must begin with repentance of this ancient error combined with a recovery of the original missionary character of the church. Hobhouse argued that mission is constitutive of the church.

In contrast to Kierkegaard's strident "Attack on Christendom," Hobhouse offered a constructive and fundamental proposal. But no one was listening, and Hobhouse's witness left no lasting impact on his own Church of England or the wider Christian movement.

Karl Barth's Conversion
from Culture Christianity

In 1909 the young Karl Barth completed his theological studies at Bern and became *pasteur suffragant* under Adolf Keller in Geneva. This was the very pulpit from which John Calvin had held sway over Geneva in the sixteenth century. Barth soon noticed that hardly anyone attended worship. He often preached to no more than a dozen people. One day while Barth was visiting an old man in the parish who was ill, he naively asked him to which church he belonged. The man responded resentfully: "Pastor, I've always been an honest man. I've never been to church and I've never been in trouble with the police" (Busch 1976:54). Barth recognized immediately that this man was representative of vast numbers of people in that society.

When Barth became pastor at Safenwil in 1911, he found the same basic pattern of scant attendance at worship services and disinterest in church religion. In this context Barth began to reconsider the "culture Christianity" in which he had been brought up and in which he had been trained. Sensing the sterility of his own message and his inability to reach his parishioners, Barth struggled to recover an experience with the God who transcends culture but meets us in our culture. From this wrestle came his powerful commentary on *The Epistle to the Romans* in 1918.[4] From this point Barth's theology was marked by a thoroughgoing theocentricism. In light of the Word of God, he critiqued the idolatry of modern culture and attacked the modern theologies that failed to do the work of exposing it. Barth's later passionate opposition to German National Socialism and his sensitivity to the demonic dimensions of modern culture become intelligible in the light of his personal encounter with the bankruptcy of Christendom at the parish level among the masses.

Cardinal Suhard and Mission to Modern Culture

When Emmanuel Suhard became Archbishop of Rheims in 1930 he observed the social and spiritual conditions of the proletarian class and was filled with alarm.[5] He concluded that the church must respond to two overriding issues: (1) the challenge of modern thought to faith and (2) the alleviation of the social and spiritual poverty that pervaded the lives of peasants and workers. Suhard rejected the view that European culture was Christian. He believed that the masses were largely outside the church, but he recognized that the traditional methods on which the church had long relied were discredited precisely with these people.

In order to know the truth of the situation, Suhard commissioned extensive surveys. These studies showed with painful clarity that France consisted of important contrasts. Certain regions of the country were functionally unchurched and resistant to the church, whereas the adjoining province or region might be a bastion of traditional Catholic religion. He learned that behind these contrasts lay important historical developments. Regions resistant to Christianity were often those that had been forcibly "Christianized." In the modern era — that is, after 1789 — they had reasserted their true colors. Their resistance was rooted in deep resentments over ancient happenings in which they perceived themselves to have been victimized by church and state.

When Suhard was created Cardinal Archbishop of Paris in 1940, he immediately turned his attention to the spiritual and social conditions of the great metropolitan area. The evident dechristianization of the metropolis shocked him. In 1942 Suhard founded the Mission de France with the intention of training missionaries for service in France. To carry out such training he established a special seminary at Lisieux. He encouraged Abbé Godin to get on with what eventually became the worker-priest movement. Godin was coauthor of the controversial book *France, A Mission Land?* published in 1943, which put forward a vision, shared by the Cardinal, for primary evangelization of France. On the wall of the Lisieux seminary refectory were written these words of Cardinal Suhard: "I have not to search for the subject of my meditation. It is always the same. There is a wall which separates the Church from the masses; the wall must be broken down at whatever cost to give back to Christ the crowds who are lost to Him."[6]

Such a mission could not, of course, be established without approval from the Vatican, but Rome was displeased with these initiatives. Only on his deathbed in May 1949 did Suhard receive from Pius XII *provisional* approval. Suhard had challenged central assumptions that undergirded Christendom; the Vatican damped down this initiative. The worker-priests became the focal point of the struggle between the French church and the Vatican.

On July 3, 1959, the Holy Office communicated to the French hierarchy the order to terminate the worker-priests. The Vatican's memorandum contained five points: "(1) The Holy See is in agreement concerning the effort that must be made to bring the laboring masses back to faith and Christian practice.... But it believes that the time-worn tradition of French Catholicism is still a considerable force toward this end. Can a country where there are still so many baptized people be considered as de-Christianized? (2) If such is the case, it is not necessary to direct priests into factory work, for there need be no modification of the traditional concept of the priesthood.... (3) Labor in factory or construction yard is incompatible with the life of a priest. ...[I]t prevents him from keeping the hours required by his obligations.... On the other hand, the influence of his surroundings must be taken into account. Not only does the priest find himself thrown into a materialistic environment (which is dangerous to his piety, perhaps even for his chastity), but he begins to think as his fellow-laborers do, to share their claims on society and to take part in the class struggle. All this is inadmissible. (4) Such an activity is permitted only to laymen. On them lies the responsibility to bring their fellow-laborers back to the Church and God.... (5) The replacement of worker-priests by new institutions will, of course, have to be carried out gradually if serious disturbance in the ministry to workers is to be avoided" (Bungener 1959:180–84). In the end the French church acquiesced to the Holy See; but in 1984 John Paul II issued a call to the Catholic faithful to share in the reevangelization of Christendom.

There is a telling footnote to this episode. In 1948 at the Katholikentag (German Catholic Church Day), a Jesuit, Father Ivo Zeiger, inspired by the Godin-Daniel book, proposed that German Catholics adopt the slogan "Germany a Missionland." But German Catholics argued that Germany could not be compared with France. Such a move would be inappropriate (Bardy 1988). Not all Germans in the post–World War II period agreed with this position, of course. Superintendent Günter Jacob at the 1956 Special Synod of the Evangelical Church in East Germany argued: "Alert minds characterize the Christian situation in Europe today in this way: that the end of the Constantinian age had arrived.... The Constantinian alliance marked the betrayal of the genuine style of the Church of Jesus Christ, which according to the view of the New Testament is to be in this world a course of suffering from the contradiction and resistance of the world. After the end of illusions about the Constantinian era, and in return to the early Christian witness, we have no right to appeal to the state for privileges and monopoly in support of the Gospel."[7] Nonetheless, this remained a minority viewpoint.

Focusing the Issue

From one viewpoint, neither John Wesley nor Cardinal Suhard stand out by virtue of the originality of their analysis of the condition of Christendom. Søren Kierkegaard and Karl Barth were not singular in their assessments of the state of the church in their respective times. The moribund and compromised condition of the church was widely acknowledged. What makes these individuals worth listening to is their passionate concern to change course.

Varied currents of renewal run through this period, extending from the Continental Pietists in the seventeenth century all the way to the worker-priests in Paris in the 1940s. Each of these renewal movements, including the worker-priests, faced official ecclesiastical censure.

The integrity of the church as the Body of Christ was believed by these prophets to be compromised at three critical points. The first was the lack of congruence between the gospel officially professed by the church and the observable low standard of Christian conduct. Whether it was the flagrant behavior of members of the university decried by Wesley or the moral nonchalance of Parson Woodforde, the lack of ethical integrity tore at the credibility of the church.

The second point, tightly bound up with the first, was that of cultural conformism. Kierkegaard fulminated against a condition where church was indistinguishable from society at large. He recognized that the very basis of the church of Christendom dictated the intertwining of church and social order. In the end this effectively silences the church. When the church has surrendered its independence, it can only echo the voice of society. And when the church no longer speaks Truth to its culture — the Word that alone can judge and transform — it becomes subject to culture. Cultural conformism ends in cultural captivity.

The third recurring theme has been the archaism of ecclesiastical structures and patterns. Effectively, the Constantinian church is controlled by the past rather than being poised to follow the Holy Spirit in responding to emerging new demands. This "morphological fundamentalism" has taken a variety of forms.[8] As a theologian Walter Hobhouse put his finger on deformed ecclesiology as the problem and urged theological reform. Cardinal Suhard and John Wesley were impelled to create new structures that would be responsive to modern industrial society in which the masses lived but from whom the church was long alienated. Both responses are required.

Lack of integrity always has an enervating effect on the church. But our account is set within a period when a wide range of new challenges were being put to the church by modern culture. It is not surprising that a church weakened at the core has been progressively marginalized over the past three centuries. The crisis of the wider culture is mirrored in the church. Poet William Butler Yeats in "The Second Coming" perceptively characterized a culture in crisis:

> Things fall apart; the centre cannot hold;
> mere anarchy is loosed upon the world . . .

The church that is no longer anchored by a convictional center that transcends culture, and which, therefore, is dependent on culture for definition, is headed for a crisis of identity. The true identity of the church will be (re)discovered in response to the presence of the kingdom of God in the lives of the people of God. No true renewal of the church is possible apart from that. A renewed church is the church of evangelical integrity.

2

Mission

In the 1930s H. Richard Niebuhr (1935), together with Wilhelm Pauck, and Francis P. Miller, wrote a tract, *The Church Against the World*. The title posits the thesis. In the introduction Niebuhr forsakes the safe haven of academe and measured scholarly argumentation. As loyal sons of the church these authors felt compelled to sound the tocsin because they found "themselves within a *threatened* [*sic*] church" (:1). Their concern arose not so much from the pressures of the world against the church as the sense that the church had lost significance. To be sure, the degree of tension between church and world varies over time, and the world will seek to seduce and convert the church in direct proportion to the intensity of the church's challenge to it. But so long as it is subservient to the world, the church will be regarded as nothing more than a fourth-rate power.

Niebuhr contended his generation now had to do with "a church which has been on the retreat and which has made compromises with the enemy in thought, in organization, and in discipline" (ibid.). The critical, saving question, insisted Niebuhr, was not whether the church measured up to social expectations. What was decisive was whether the church was being true to itself and its head. Thus the insistent self-addressed question was: "What must we do to be saved?" (:2). For the church "to be saved" it must embrace its full ecclesial identity and turn its back on its idolization of worldly systems of power and thought. When this is done the church assumes a redemptive role in relation to the world.

One of the urgent themes in 1935 — as in the 1990s — was the self-evident peril confronting civilization and its institutions. From many sides the church was being urged to make itself relevant to this world in crisis by adjusting to modern realities. But this appeal must not be answered simplistically. "The desire to become all things to all men still presupposes a faith which does not change and a gospel to which they are to be won" (:11). The essential problem was that the church had so accommodated to the world that the world's crisis had become the church's crisis. The church lacked the will and the insight to discern the times and choose for God, thereby saying no to the false gods.

The relationship between church and world should be visualized as two systems, suggested Niebuhr, each of which is in continuous motion. The church-world nexus itself ranges from separation to symbiotic relationship. "A converted church in a corrupt civilization" (:123) is strongly aware of its identity and does not depend on the world to sustain it. Its identity as the people called to live out God's reign becomes the indispensable resource. This pristine identity will issue in a vigorous evangelization of its culture. As people embrace the faith, this initial rigorism gradually yields to a more pastoral outlook. This leads to the development of working arrangements with the powers and institutions of society and the visible lessening of tension between church and society. The result, as trenchantly summarized by Niebuhr, is that "faith loses its force ... discipline is relaxed, repentance grows formal, corruption enters with idolatry, and the church, tied to culture which it sponsored, suffers corruption with it" (ibid.). The hope for recovery of its true character is for the church to return to its origins and start the process over again. "Only a new withdrawal followed by a new aggression can then save the church and restore to it the salt with which to savor society" (ibid.). A compromised church is a church that has surrendered its mission. The criterion by which we may judge the recovery of the church's identity is whether the church has a restored missional consciousness.

Niebuhr observed that historically the church has passed through three such cycles, with the most recent one occurring in the modern period. "The task of the present generation," he declared, "appears to lie in the liberation of the church from its bondage to a corrupt civilization" (1:24). That liberation will come about by the positive rediscovery of the church's primordial purpose. The church is truly free when it embraces its calling fully.

The nagging historical question is why the many renewal movements, starting with the Pietists, have failed to change the church at the core. A range of reform efforts in the modern era, including the Pietist-Evangelical Revival on the one side and liturgical-ritual reform on the other, have not availed to deliver the church from enfeebling compromise.

The thesis to be tested here is that the church was instituted for the service of the *missio Dei,* and this remains its essential purpose. However, the church of modern Western culture lives out of the inheritance of Christendom, a church severed from mission. Renewal that does not result in a church renewed in mission is not genuine. The sole source for renewal of the church is the *missio Dei* as the basis for its life in relationship to the world.

The Christendom Model

Christendom has been the prevailing model of church since the fourth century. Historical Christendom was the powerful religio-political synthesis that resulted when Christianity won recognition as the religion of state in the fourth century. Increasingly, the church now took its place alongside the other powers controlling society but was thus itself redefined by its new role.

The transformation of the church from persecuted minority to official religion fundamentally altered the relationship of the church to the sociopolitical order. The understanding of the church's mission, its *raison d'être*, was altered. Christendom politicized mission by making it an instrument of state policy. It was now the "mission" of church and state to ensure that all inhabitants of the empire were Christian. Once the tribes of Europe had been pacified and brought under control there was no further need for even this politicized mission.

The notion of *apostolic* mission within the territory of Christendom contradicted the meaning of this new society.[1] The territory of Christendom was sacralized; it was the new Holy Land. Christendom fused the religious and the political. Citizenship was established at baptism, and the church regulated the life of the citizenry on behalf of both church and state. As a result of these developments, the church surrendered the vital critical relationship to its culture that is indispensable to a sense of mission.

An important permutation of mission did emerge in the fifteenth century. In conjunction with the sending out of the Portuguese and Spanish trading expeditions, the Pope authorized the crowns of Portugal and Spain to dispatch these expeditions with the proviso that priests be included to provide spiritual care of Europeans who populated the trading colonies and to do missionary work among the native inhabitants. This powerful bonding between missions and trading expeditions to foreign lands has held firm right up to modern times. And this paradigm reinforced the notion that missions are unidirectional, from Christendom to heathendom.

However, it is not claiming too much to say that, in the end, this permutation, unsatisfactory as it was, would contribute to the dissolution of historical Christendom and helped set the stage for the church to reclaim its missional identity. The modern mission movement, a direct result of the Pietist-Evangelical Revival, represents the full flowering of this particular variety of mission. Although the Protestant promoters of missions in the first years of the modern movement did not have the approval of most church leaders, they persisted. By 1850 missions were generally accepted as a "duty" of the Christian church. This turned the attention of the churches outward. Consequently, new churches were being established in many countries where there had been no Christian activity before — that is, beyond the boundaries of Christendom. Traditional assumptions about Christian faith and practice began to be tested in these many new environments. The historic churches of Christendom were thus experiencing, once again, the demands made as a result of participation in mission. These testings led to adaptations that departed from Christendom patterns based on a *missional* rather than *pastoral* perspective. Notwithstanding these experiences in the past two hundred years, the ecclesial identity of the church in the West has not been deeply affected by mission. The mission dynamic was allowed free rein only beyond the pale of Christendom.

The Christendom model of church may be characterized as *church without mission.* We therefore hypothesize that if the starting point is a flawed model of church, that is to say, a model lacking theological and conceptual integrity, then attempts to revive or renew the church within this fundamentally deficient model cannot be expected to result in fundamental and long-term change.

The Legacy of the Sixteenth-Century Reformation

What ignited the witness of Martin Luther, making it the catalyst for the Reformation, was his own testimony to the power of God's forgiveness and justification by faith that he personally experienced. The initiative rests with a gracious and just God rather than a corrupt and fallible ecclesiastical system. Luther's experience found resonance among large numbers of people for whom the traditional church did not have a satisfying answer. Luther's account of his Damascus Road experience became definitive among Protestants. Luther had uncovered the importance of the biblical doctrine of justification by faith as the spiritual foundation of personal identity and responsibility. One immediate result was the articulation of the revolutionary theme of the priesthood of all believers within a church subject to continual reform. Luther emphasized the authority of the Word. He further broke with church convention by producing a highly successful translation of the Bible in the German vernacular.

These developments ineluctably drove Luther to face the question of the nature of the church. Against the background of the ecclesial reality he wanted to see reformed, Martin Luther described the ideal church in terms of the following seven characteristics: (1) voluntary membership; (2) a covenanted community; (3) a lifestyle marked by ethical seriousness; (4) disciplined congregations; (5) fraternal economic practices; (6) liturgy in the vernacular which is simple and functional; (7) authoritative scriptural word mediated through the Holy Spirit (Lehmann 1965:64; Driver 1979:1; Durnbaugh 1968:1, 32). This is a remarkable statement. Each point is, in fact, a critical response to prevailing ecclesiastical patterns and practices.[2] Luther himself had no confidence in effectuating such a change in church life, however. He remarked that "if one had the kind of people and persons who wanted to be Christians in earnest, the rules and regulations would soon be ready.... I have not yet the people or persons for it, nor do I see many who want it" (Lehmann ibid.). Luther concluded he had to settle for something less.

In his illuminating comparative study of Luther and the Latin American Base Ecclesial Communities, Richard Shaull (1991:4f) argues that in the end the promise of Luther's Reformation turned to ashes. In the first place, Luther did not give sufficient guidance as to how the results of spiritual transformation are to be applied in the socio-political sphere. Second, Luther wavered on the matter of the relation of church to state and, in the end, settled for a

continuation of the old state church system. A third failure
was Luther's decision not to take the side of the people in
the Peasants' War of 1524–26, thus confirming the impression that the church was always on the side of the state.
Fourth, Luther's grand vision of a church open to continual reform was never realized. Instead, the Reformation
churches settled into an institutional neo-Christendom.

There is a long tradition of scholarly debate as to
whether or not the leading Protestant Reformers of the sixteenth century were advocates for missions (cf. Yoder 1984).
It is largely an empty exercise whereby twentieth-century
questions are forced on the sixteenth century. Whether one
were Catholic or Protestant,[3] missions within Christendom
had no place theologically or ecclesiastically; and Protestant
Europe had not yet embarked on colonial expansion in the
manner of the Catholic Portuguese and Spanish.

Stephen Neill (1968:71–77) has demonstrated how the
power of tradition, reinforced by the immediate religio-
political context, decisively shaped the ecclesiology of the
sixteenth century. Neill has compared the official confessional statements of the Anglican, Roman Catholic,
Lutheran, and Reformed traditions of the sixteenth century
with reference to the nature of the church. For example, the
Augsburg Confession of 1530 states:

> Moreover, they teach that one holy Church is to re-
> main in perpetuity. The Church is the congregation
> of the saints in which the Gospel is purely taught, and
> the sacraments are rightly administered (:71f).

The confessional statements of the other three traditions strike the same stance: all emphasize the *being* rather
than the *function* of the church. Ecclesiologically the church

is turned inward. The thrust of these statements, which were the very basis for catechizing and guiding the faithful, rather than equipping and mobilizing the church to engage the world, was to guard and preserve. This is altogether logical, of course, if the whole of society is by definition already under the lordship of Christ. Theologically and practically, the kingdom of God is treated as being coextensive with the church, and, in turn, church and society are indistinguishable.

The Church of Christendom and Modern Culture

Throughout the nineteenth century, with the whole of culture increasingly dominated by science, technology, and industrialization, the church was on the defensive. Antagonists of the Christian faith such as Thomas Huxley played science off against religion and successfully discredited the church in the popular mind. Given its role throughout the history of Christendom as ally of the civil powers, the established church had difficulty establishing credibility with the masses. Well aware of the alienation between the masses and the church, Pius XI admitted that "the greatest scandal of the Church in the nineteenth century was that it lost the working class" (Gilbert 1976; McLeod 1981). It was one thing to recognize the situation for what it was but quite another matter to mount a response. The churches chose to maintain the status quo.[4]

Living conditions in the burgeoning industrial towns of the nineteenth century were notoriously bad. Exploitation of the working class by the industrial machine was only partially mitigated by social reforms and the organization of labor unions. By the start of the twentieth century the division between working class and the rest of society was firmly fixed.

The modern period was marked by another process that had far-reaching implications for the church. Dietrich Bonhoeffer identified the controlling assumption of modern culture to be that humankind had "come of age," meaning that the modern human had outgrown the need for religion. In the years following World War II, Europe was frequently described as a post-Christian society. The triumph of secularization came to be regarded as inevitable and irreversible. By the 1960s theologians were reinterpreting the Christian message in the light of secularization. Harvey Cox (1965:4) caught the mood of the times in his bestseller *The Secular City:* "Secularization rolls on, and if we are to understand and communicate with our present age we must learn to love it in its unremitting secularity." The message, which had almost become a taunt, was clear: any peace settlement between church/religion and culture would be on terms set by secular culture.

This triumphalist interpretation of secularization, driven by an ideological secularism, was not accepted by everyone, of course. For those who looked at the evidence with discrimination, signs of religious devotion were to be found on all sides, including the places where there was supposed to be none, such as rapidly modernizing Japan. Secularization had to be redefined (Bruce 1992; Hammond 1985).

The phenomenon of secularization was real, but the picture was confusing. Although traditional symbols and rituals were losing their significance for large numbers of people, new forms of religion and new symbols were appearing, some bizarre and esoteric, to be sure. It was the long-established churches and synagogues that were struggling against decline.

The North American situation was different from Europe's, where formal religious practice had shrunk steadily throughout most of the twentieth century. But in the 1970s several studies of the weakening position of mainline churches in the United States were published. In *Why Conservative Churches Are Growing*, Dean M. Kelley (1972) argued that people embrace a religious movement because it helps them make sense of life and because it imposes demands on its adherents. The mainline churches were losing adherents as a result of their failure to "stand for something" other than general cultural values. Kelley contrasted the lax standards of membership of the mainline churches with the more strict, and growing, conservative churches. It was a controversial thesis and oversimplified the facts in certain ways. But subsequent testing of the Kelley thesis confirmed that on the main points he was correct (Hoge 1979; Roof 1979). Secularization and cultural accommodation do correlate directly with decline in the strength and vitality of the church.

As already noted, secularization theories were inadequate to account for all the data at hand. Modern culture was irrepressibly religious but often antagonistic toward Christianity. Could it be that, in reacting to religion, secular culture actually contributed to the rise of new religions? Peter Berger proposed a provocative hypothesis: *The current occult wave (including its devil component) is to be understood as resulting from the repression of transcendence in modern consciousness* (Berger 1979:255). The secularization process in fact had a twin called sacralization. Although the church bore the brunt of secularization — measured in terms of spreading malaise and declining membership — it figured only marginally in the new sacralization that was taking place in modern culture. Thus the Christian church seemed to be the big loser on most fronts (cf. Marsden and Longfield 1992).

The church does not exist in the abstract. It is a visible, living reality. Whether one speaks of the church local or universal, one is describing an empirical reality. The genius of Christian faith is that it must become vernacularized. The faithful church *in situ* has no choice but to work out its life within a culture; and it must, therefore, come to terms with the plausibility structure of that culture. The question is whether it will allow itself to be molded to fit this structure or do the hard work of discerning how it will live in redemptive tension with it. The modern plausibility structure sought to exclude religion altogether. Accommodation to such a plausibility framework would assuredly spell trouble, if not the end of the church. However, certain theologians have advocated just such a move on the part of the church.

Because the church of post-Enlightenment Christendom has had a truncated integrity — that is, in critical ways its identity was defined by culture rather than by the gospel — it has lacked a sense of *missional responsibility* to its culture. Indeed, the dominant model — which was protested periodically by various dissenting movements — was that of collaboration with culture. Had the church understood itself as having a mission to culture, it would perforce have engaged modern culture in light of the reign of God. Modern culture guided by and based on the philosophy of the Enlightenment proposed a set of assumptions that impinge on human welfare and destiny. These issues deserved a searching rejoinder rather than merely an echo of culture's own voice.

The Contribution of Theologians

Surveys of the agenda that preoccupied theologians over the past three centuries indicate that ecclesiology was largely absent until the twentieth century. The ecumenical councils that met from time to time between the fourth and eighth centuries did not deal with the nature of the church. George H. Tavard reports that within the Roman Catholic tradition apparently no direct address of ecclesiology was made until Vatican I, in 1870, when the dogmatic constitution, *Pastor aeternus,* was introduced. Even then it was discussion of structure, rather than the nature of the church, that preoccupied the church's theologians. Roman Catholic ecclesiological studies began to flourish in the midtwentieth century, a development that contributed substantially to the work of Vatican II, 1962–65 (Tavard 1992:7–13; Dulles 1989; Donovan 1977).

During the same period the situation among Protestants has been essentially the same. Ecclesiology was not a priority interest among theologians until Karl Barth entered the scene in the twentieth century and began writing his massive *Church Dogmatics.*[5] But the church as a theological concern has remained a secondary interest within the enterprise as a whole.

If ecclesiology has been largely stored in the pantry of the house built by theologians, mission hardly got a foot in the door. David J. Bosch (1972; 1982) repeatedly challenged this bias against mission on the part of the professional theologians, citing the aphorism of the German systematic theologian, Martin Kaehler (d. 1911): "Mission is the mother of theology." Kaehler argued that the model for theological work found in the New Testament presupposes missionary engagement. New Testament theology is developed in response to the knotty questions being thrown up as the Christian witness engages the plurality of cultures and religions of the Mediterranean world of that time. New Testament theology is essentially the working out of the ecclesial reality in the local interface between church and world. By contrast, the theology of Roman Catholic and Protestant theologians in the modern period has been geared to maintaining the continuity of the Christendom tradition — which, as we have already noted, has set mission aside. Clear evidence of this bias is the fact that theologians have ignored the modern missionary movement, choosing instead to maintain a steady provincial and intramural focus.

Mission Constitutive of Church

Christians living in modern culture face a fundamental challenge. That challenge is to learn to think about their culture in missional terms. We have sought to demonstrate how the patterns and habits of thought that determine our attitudes and outlook vis-à-vis our culture have been formed over a period of some fifteen hundred years. Whether one has been reared in an established church or a free or nonconformist church, Christendom has been the powerful overshadowing influence.

Furthermore, we can acknowledge with gratitude that many Christians have already made serious attempts to come to terms with modern culture in ways both positive and negative. They can teach us certain important lessons. Here we will consider briefly two such attempts.

Theological liberalism became an important influence in the church in the nineteenth century. By 1900 "modernism," a child of liberalism, emerged on the scene, especially in North America. William R. Hutchison (1982:2) has characterized modernism in terms of three features: "First and most visibly, it meant the conscious, intended adaptation of religious ideas to modern culture.... [T]wo further and deeper notions were important. One was the idea that God is immanent in human cultural development and revealed through it. The other was a belief that human society is moving toward realization... of the Kingdom of God." As Hutchison makes clear, this tradition was always ambivalent about the idea of mission, continuing to champion the ideal of adaptation to culture and maintaining vigilance against any action that suggested "dogma." This tradition held firmly to the ideal whereby the church collaborated as closely as possible with culture in its goal of realizing the kingdom of God on earth. The liberal mission was *in* rather than *to* culture.

After World War I a number of theologians who had identified with liberalism broke away and became major critics of liberalism, which had allied itself so tightly to modern culture that it had little to say to a culture that was now in deep crisis. This movement of reaction came to be known as neoorthodoxy. Neoorthodox theologians such as Karl Barth, Emil Brunner, and Reinhold Niebuhr spoke with authority and power as they critiqued the present situation — especially the rise of National Socialism — in light of the Word of God and called for repentance. Uncritical accommodation has little potential for engendering witness that moves against the cultural mainstream.

Another movement that emerged at the start of the twentieth century was what became known as fundamentalism. It was a direct response to modernism and thus to modernity. Viscerally opposed to modernism, fundamentalists saw themselves as holding back the floodwaters of modernity. They rejected the modernists' attempts to adapt religion to modern culture. Fundamentalists expressed their opposition to culture, in part, by promoting traditional Christian missions. Fundamentalists based their reaction to modernists and the Social Gospel on a premillennial/dispensational eschatology with its emphasis on the futility of improving conditions in this world. Rather, they emphasized preaching an evangelistic gospel in order to save souls for heaven. One mark of their opposition to modernism and the Social Gospel was to distance themselves from advocacy of social service ministries and to insist on evangelism as their priority. With their truncated gospel and culture-rejecting outlook, these fundamentalists had little to say to the crisis in modern culture other than to decry the situation. As George Marsden (1980: 11–21) has demonstrated, fundamentalist attitudes were imbued with Enlightenment values, which ostensibly they were protesting against.

We have been arguing, implicitly, that the church is true to its nature — and thus possesses integrity — when it understands itself to be God's missionary presence in the world. Neither the modernist drive to adapt faith to culture nor the early fundamentalist escapist message provides us with a usable model. These two responses to modern culture afford us no constructive clues as to how the church as

Christ's body is to be present in culture, for neither has a sense of missional responsibility to culture.

It is instructive that when our Lord began his public ministry he declared his originating assumption with stark simplicity: "The time is fulfilled, and the kingdom of God has come near; repent, and believe in the good news" (Mark 1:15). The ministry of Jesus was set within the culture in which he was born and reared. With rare penetration he grasped the presuppositions on which his own culture rested. He attacked the religious legalism that could not mediate God's saving and gracious presence to the people. He undermined the power system based on rank and position by calling for servanthood among his followers. Jesus made love of God and neighbor the central requirements of faith rather than ritual observance. Even his response to people set a new pattern. Consider the probing questions he put to people and the parables he told in reply to their questions. His ministry was notable for the way he engaged what mattered most to people. For example, when he "talked about the weather" he penetrated the cultural substratum, that is, their anxiety about the future.

The Palestine of Jesus' time was a culture in turmoil and under great strain. It was nearing the breaking point as the Jewish people suffered under the Roman occupation, while at the same time the Jewish community was riven by deep internal divisions. Jesus modeled for us what it means to be in missionary encounter with one's culture. He approached the culture of his day with infinite compassion and courageous truth telling. The stance of Jesus was not that of rejecting his culture; rather, he started where people were and pointed them to life renewed through God's loving redemptive power.

Jesus was the outsider who became the insider without surrendering his outsider status. He never relaxed this bifocal stance. Jesus was recognizably "their own," but they refused to "own" him (John 1:9–14). He represented to his people God's *basileia*, source both of judgment and hope. They recognized that in him they were encountering the truth both about God and themselves. In his incarnation Jesus held together his full identification with the human situation and his uncompromising commitment to God's *basileia*. This was the force field out of which his extraordinary mission emanated. And every clue Jesus gave his disciples as to their own missionary vocation suggests that this is the authoritative model for them as well. Jesus left no general guidelines, formulae, or methods for his disciples to follow; only a demanding model.

Based on this model, we can make several observations with reference to our situation today. First, this model calls us to reject the Christendom notion whereby we claim any culture as being fully "Christian." Every culture is incomplete without the gospel, but no culture is ever completely evangelized. That is to say, no culture is wholly submitted to the reign of God. Because the church should know its own culture best, it has a special missionary vocation to that culture. Significantly, the Great Commission includes all arenas of human life and activity in the mandate of the church, a point to be developed further in Chapter 4. At no point is the church given license to stop thinking in missionary terms.

A second observation is that the church's normal relationship to every culture is that of missionary encounter. The faithful church living out God's reign cannot feel completely at home in any culture; yet in light of God's *basileia* the church is responsible to witness to God's saving intention in every society. This calls the church to a twofold action in relation to all cultures. Incarnation signifies full identification, but it is incarnation in the service of the disclosure of God's love and will for humankind. The revealing of God's will brings human behavior under judgment and always results in agitated reaction. This is the way marked by the cross. The faithful witnessing church will, therefore, present a contrast to the surrounding culture and must expect to live in tension with the larger culture and possibly endure hostility.

Third, there is no biblical or theological basis for the territorial distinction between mission and evangelization. To accede to this dichotomy is to invite the church to "settle in" and be at home. The church is most at risk where it has been present in a culture for a long period of time so that it no longer conceives its relation to culture in terms of missionary encounter. The church remains socially and salvifically relevant only so long as it is in redemptive tension with culture.

These three points are made over against the tradition of Christendom with its inbred resistance to mission to its own culture. A church conformed, and conforming, to the will of God is one that lives in consciousness of its missional nature. Mission is the motor that drives the church in obedient response to the reign of God in the world. "But you are a chosen race, a royal priesthood, a holy nation, God's own people, in order that you may proclaim the mighty acts of him who called you out of darkness into his marvelous light" (1 Pet. 2:9).

The Ambiguous Role of Missiologists

In that period of remarkable flowering of missionary interest and activity between 1786 and 1825, both missionary societies and mission training institutions were founded on the Continent, the British Isles, and North America. Mission training was understood to consist of the equipping of missionary candidates with the necessary practical knowledge for cross-cultural service. By the end of the first generation, pleas began to be voiced for more rigorous mission studies. William Orme (1828), secretary of the London Missionary Society, in 1828 pleaded for a "philosophy of missions." By 1850 the term "science of missions" was being used, but mission studies still had no home.

The "Plan for a Theological Seminary" adopted by the Presbyterian General Assembly in 1811 included in its purpose: "to found a nursery for missionaries to the heathen, and to such as are destitute of the stated preaching of the Gospel: in which youth may receive that appropriate training which may lay a foundation for their ultimately becoming eminently qualified for missionary work" (Myklebust 1957:I:146). Although Princeton Theological Seminary was soon established, mission training was not introduced until the 1830s when Charles Breckenridge was appointed to the chair of Pastoral Theology and Missionary Instruction. When Breckenridge became Presbyterian Mission Board secretary in 1839, no replacement was appointed. Instead courses were taught by other faculty members until the courses were dropped from the curriculum in 1855. Several other abortive efforts were made in the British Isles and on the Continent in the 1860s to bring mission studies into theological faculties.[6]

It took the long and heroic exertions of Gustav Warneck, pioneer German missiologist, finally to get mission studies admitted to the university curriculum at the end of the nineteenth century. The academy made no effort to conceal its ambivalence about this development. Nonetheless, this does mark a certain coming of age of mission studies with chairs in missions or missiology being added in a considerable number of seminaries and faculties of theology across Europe and in North America after 1900.

The modern mission enterprise rested on the premise that its task was the extension of Christendom worldwide. This premise went unexamined for several generations. That it was foundational to mission studies can be demonstrated by the monumental contribution of Gustav Warneck. One of the articles of faith for Warneck, and widely adopted by others, was to contrast *missions* and *evangelization* stereotypically based on Christendom assumptions.[7] Warneck insisted that missions were activities conducted beyond the bounds of historical Christendom with the goal of establishing the church where it had not been before. On the other hand, evangelization was the action of the church to bring nominal Christians to vital faith. This formulation remained influential in missiological theory until after 1945.

This distinction between mission and evangelization, with mission directed to heathendom and evangelization associated with Christendom, was a construct that could not be explained or supported exegetically. Its justification arose in defense of historical Christendom. If one subjects it to theological critique, it cannot stand. Neither the New Testament nor the early church resorted to such a dichotomy. Furthermore, the mission dynamic operating in the modern mission movement beyond the bounds of historical

Christendom contributed to the dissolution of Christendom, both as an ideal and as a historical reality, through the recovery of missionary action by the church.

During the 1950s and early 1960s a spate of books appeared on the "crisis" facing missions. The closing of China to Western missions in 1949 intensified the sense of crisis but kept the focus on "foreign" missions (Paton 1953). Although the "crisis of the church" in the West was acknowledged, this was treated as a pastoral problem. No missiologist addressed the question of mission to the West or challenged the assumption that the crisis in the West might also be a crisis of a church that had lost its mission. Mission studies remained firmly tied to the cross-cultural questions that had been their staple since the beginning of modern missions.

A conceptual shift was intimated by the theme adopted by the Commission on World Mission and Evangelism (CWME) of the World Council of Churches at its meeting in Mexico City in 1963: "Mission from six continents to six continents." The CWME followed up with a study in Europe and North America of "the missionary structure of the congregation," an initiative that never fulfilled its promise.[8] At the same time Vatican Council II was forging a new position for Roman Catholics that emphasized the missionary responsibility of the whole people of God. But the conceptual innovation has yet to be translated into reforms — whether ecclesial, missiological, or in theological education.

The problematic had various dimensions. Two centuries of worldwide missionary exertions sponsored by Western churches had largely failed to effect a fundamental reorientation in their ecclesial consciousness. In terms of that consciousness, Christendom remained a self-sufficient and insular reality. Church history and theology continued to be taught in the West as a Western affair. What happened "out there" was missions and therefore of no immediate consequence; what happened in the West was "church." For example, Owen Chadwick's authoritative two-volume study of *The Victorian Church* — the period when British missions had the largest missionary contingent of any nationality — contained not a single reference to this movement (Walls 1991:146). Yet his own Anglican communion was an outstanding example of how the empirical reality of church had been drastically changed by missionary pioneering in the nineteenth century.

Few missiologists have challenged this state of affairs. Christendom assumptions and habits of mind have continued to determine the conceptual framework even among those who have participated in global mission and were trained to think in critical, comparative, and comprehensive terms. This represents an important dimension of the re-visioning that must take place.

3

Evangelization

The New Testament recounts the original evangelization.[1]
Based on this rendering, we can make several observations.
In the first place, evangelization has been controversial from
the beginning. The message of Jesus stirred strong reactions
in his contemporaries. Some warmed to what they heard.
Others were deeply threatened by his words. The witness
of the first apostles engendered the same reaction. Their
contemporaries charged them with upsetting the world, a
charge that was undoubtedly true, for as a result of their
preaching people turned against the accepted ways of their
culture in response to a new authority. The apostolic witness resulted in disruption of socioeconomic structures and
inspired people to give their highest allegiance to Jesus the
Messiah rather than Caesar. Throughout the history of the
church evangelization has remained a contentious issue —
both between church and society as well as within the
church itself.

A closely related second observation is that the evangel
in the New Testament era threw a searching light on the
human condition located within the religio-cultural context of that time. That is, it was a message that confronted

and exposed the regnant worldview and the ways in which people were held hostage by a corrupt and ill-fated system. This confrontation begins with Jesus' temptation in the wilderness and subsequently becomes the focal point of his public ministry. Indeed, he begins that ministry with the announcement: "The time is fulfilled and the kingdom of God has come near, repent, and believe in the good news" (Mark 1:15). It addressed each individual, to be sure, but the individual in responsible relationship to the sociohistorical context.

Third, the message of Jesus was invitational, and not only confrontational. Having exposed the situation by speaking truth, Jesus put a genuine choice before all who came to him. The world was in bondage, with no possibility of freeing itself, but God offered liberation. That liberation was taking form in response to God's reign that was now becoming a reality. "Repent," that is, "turn around," urged Jesus, and move into God's light and life.

The church's understanding of itself, the gospel, and the world is always reflected in the content and manner of its evangelization. At no other point does the church place itself so openly at cross-purposes with the world than when it announces that this present order has no efficacious answer to human destiny. If the church, under the inspiration of its head, Jesus Christ, lives by the conviction that the world is on a course that leads to death, it has no other choice than to invite men and women to become a part of God's new order, the kingdom of life. The church that is not evangelizing is a church that does not truly believe the gospel. It is a faithless church.

Faithful evangelization, drawing as it must on the message and tradition of the ancient Hebrew prophets, is unavoidably crisis producing. Prophetic evangelization gets to the heart of matters and lays bare the injustice and evil that mark personal and social relations. It will challenge human propensities and personal loyalties at the deepest levels because it exposes the contrast between God's gracious action in our behalf and our motives and drives. Witness to God's grace is invitational.

There are other reasons that account for the fact that evangelization is controversial. Evangelists are invariably fallible humans, flawed earthen vessels who leave their own fingerprints on the message. A gracious God has chosen to entrust to imperfect humans the privilege of evangelizing. As with all things good, the gospel can be handled in ways that cheapen or betray it, discrediting both the individual and the Christian community and intensifying resistance to evangel and evangelist.

The modern period has seen the rise of a new kind of evangelization through the influence of powerful pulpiteers — Whitefield, the Wesleys, Finney, Moody, Graham, to name only a few — who have created new vocabulary, methods, and message, and turned evangelization into a specialized ministry largely separated from the church. Equally important, the evangelistic enterprise has emerged within Enlightenment culture with its public/private dichotomy, with religion consigned to the private sphere. Theologically and methodologically, it has been assumed that the main point of concentration is the individual and the sins of the flesh. The overall effect has been reductionist. By effectively limiting the evangel to the personal, evangelization has foreclosed on prophetic witness, which always challenges the present categories; evangelization encompasses both the private and the public, the individual and the social. Unless the gospel engages the whole of human reality — starting with the prevailing worldview — it is a scaled-down gospel.

What we are concerned with here, however, is not the Elmer Gantry caricature of the evangelist that has had such wide play in contemporary culture. Rather, this is a call to understand the more subtle ways in which the gospel can be subverted. *We hypothesize that the church in modern culture has succumbed to syncretism in pursuit of evangelization by its uncritical appropriation of the assumptions and methodologies offered by modern culture.*

Evangelization and Modern Culture

A cursory survey of works on evangelization that have been produced over the past century, from a range of ecclesiastical traditions, reveals a telling pattern. The vast majority are devoted to methods and techniques of evangelism. Rarely does one find a work that has approached the evangelistic task biblically and theologically (Abraham 1989; Costas 1989). Evangelization has been understood as Practical Theology. Fundamental theological questions could be bracketed. The immediate task was to work out questions of "application" rather than the need to wrestle continually with the biblical/theological grounding, on the one hand, and the gospel in relation to culture, on the other. It should be noted that the watermark of modern culture is *technique*. Modern evangelization is thoroughly modern in concept and practice. None of these works subjects evangelistic methods and techniques to theological scrutiny. On the contrary, there is an uncritical reliance on such props.

One of the major influences in adapting evangelization to modern culture has been Charles Grandison Finney (1792–1875), preeminent American evangelist in the first half of the nineteenth century. A practicing lawyer at the time of his conversion, Finney entered the Christian ministry without benefit of formal theological training. "I was bred a lawyer," he said. "I came forth from a law office to the pulpit, and talked to the people as I would talk to a jury." Perry Miller (1966:25) commented: "He wanted decisions, here and now, not in some endless metaphysical realm.... What is fascinating about him is that he is not a bully, but the advocate at the bar." Finney's methods were the subject of intense controversy from the outset, and not only because of his strong personality (Hardman 1990:chaps. 5, 8). Finney wrought a sea change in evangelization.

All evangelists of the period were passionate and strong personalities. "But as compared with Finney, they all seem pallid," noted Perry Miller (1966:23f). This was because "all the others, whether in Connecticut or Kentucky, were linked with the eighteenth century, striving to enact anew the Great Awakening of 1740. Finney's preeminence lies in his embracing the Revival out of no academic theological training, but fully imbued with the spirit of the nineteenth century.... Finney among the evangelicals was a Napoleon among his marshals.... He imposed 'new measures.' Finney 'prolonged' his meetings, not only into the small hours of the morning, but for day after day, so that all business was brought to a standstill. More outrageously, he had the unconverted in every town he visited prayed for 'by name.' He allowed women to pray in public. Above all he devised the 'anxious bench'...a space kept empty in front of the meeting, to which penitents could walk (or stumble) in full view of the society, and there be interrogated, criminals on their own admission, by God's attorney, Charles Grandison Finney" (ibid.). The evangelist now became the bold innovative entrepreneur.

Accepting Miller's assessment, Keith Hardman (1990: 99) argues further that Finney to a degree not matched by his fellow evangelists personified "the activism of the period of Jacksonian democracy in America," and his approach was attuned to the cultural mood, not least the strong millennial expectation. According to Ernest R. Sandeen (1978:42), "America in the early nineteenth century was drunk on the millennium." At the founding meeting of the Evangelical Alliance in London in 1846, Samuel H. Cox, moderator of the Presbyterian Church that year, with ill-concealed chauvinism, declared: "[I]n America, the state of society is without parallel in universal history. With all our mixtures, there is a leaven of heaven; there is goodness there; there is excellent principle there. I really believe that God has got America within anchorage, and that upon that arena, He intends to display his prodigies for the millennium" (ibid.). Cox's rhetoric was common coinage. Finney shared fully this optimistic millennial vision. He "pictured America as the coming center of a divinely ordered universe, with God as its governor, the people as his obedient subjects, and the eternal law of benevolence as its guiding light" (Rosell 1984:142). Breaking with his Calvinist past, Finney argued that it was the duty of Christians to prepare society for the millennium by collaborating with God. This issued in a powerful call to hasten the coming millennial reign through personal and social renovation. Many of Finney's converts became active in various reform efforts with a view to making America a Christian society.

The Revival had gained sufficient momentum that by the second decade of the nineteenth century the future of the American republic was being linked to revivalism. This was based on a new formulation. In the 1840s the term *conservative* was introduced to describe this special relationship wherein Christianity was the "true conserving and developing power of a nation" (Miller 1966:70; see "This Nation Under God," 66–72). Revivals were viewed as the energizer of Christianity, ensuring it would not fail in its duty to society. Increasingly, after 1865 this fostered in revivalists an attitude of protectiveness toward society generally, in contrast to particular ills, and social quietism rather than prophetic scrutiny.

Finney's success as an evangelist could be attributed to a combination of personal charisma, spiritual passion, entrepreneurial skill, and cultural fit. Finney underscored the importance of appropriating whatever means might enhance the work of the revivalist. Unlike evangelists in the 150 years since his heyday, Finney wrote extensively on the theory and practice of revivals. During his years as a professor of theology he also produced a three-volume work, *Lectures on Systematic Theology*, which buttressed his vision of an activist faith.

Finney's life and work are important to our analysis for several reasons. His career marks the beginning of the most influential type of modern evangelist, especially in North America. Although Finney succeeded in being credentialed as an ordained Presbyterian minister, he never completely shed his image as the layman who assumed the mantle of evangelist without the full blessing of the church, and his relations with the institutional church were frequently stormy. Many other evangelists have followed in

Finney's train, that is, conducting their evangelistic work independent of the church. Of greater importance is Finney's strong reliance on technique and method. Under his influence evangelization became more firmly identified as essentially a matter of technique. This points to a third facet, namely, the way Finney reflected nineteenth-century American culture, the period of a new populism known as Jacksonian democracy. Finney did indeed bring a critique to bear on society, but it is critique wholly from within — in contrast to that of Jesus, which was both from within and without. Finney's view of culture was that of Christendom, which predisposed him to embrace much of the culture of his day. He, of course, struggled against secular incursions into religious life and influence and looked forward to the day when America would be fully Christian.

Both as the leading evangelist and the most prolific writer on evangelization in the midnineteenth century, Charles G. Finney left a standard against which to compare subsequent writings on evangelization. Although many volumes have been written in the intervening years, modern revival theory and practice have not seriously engaged the controlling worldview of modern culture. The focus has remained almost entirely on the individual and personal morality.

The way the church understands the world and the relationship between the two is decisive. For an outstanding example of one who understood the importance of coming to grips with the presuppositional foundation of modern culture, we turn to Peter Taylor Forsyth (1848–1921), whose theology anticipated in important ways that of Karl Barth and the Theology of Crisis in the next generation. Forsyth argued that the church must work out a basic stance vis-à-vis culture that would enable it to avoid slipping into complicity with culture. He observed that "in the great and crucial ages of the Church she saved herself and her word by taking the attitude of detachment . . . rather than accommodation. . . . She served a world she would not obey, in the name of a mastery it could neither confer nor withstand."[2] The church must preserve this independence precisely in order to play the role in the world's salvation to which it was appointed by its head, Jesus Christ.

One explanation for the perennial lack of attention (*pace* Forsyth and others) both to theology and cultural context may be found in the traditional distinction between mission, the church's action directed to foreign lands, and evangelization, which takes place within Christian culture. As pointed out earlier, this understanding is rooted in historical Christendom. Evangelization had a prescribed meaning in relation to the masses of nominal Christians whose latent faith needed to be enlivened. Evangelization was an activity to be conducted in a culture that the church insisted was already, in some sense, "Christian." In light of this assumption, it made sense to speak of "revival," vivifying the spiritually moribund without radical critique of their worldview and the structures of their society.

A second explanation arises from the way fundamental assumptions of modern culture have been incorporated into Christian theology and practice. One of the most important contributions made by the Enlightenment to modern culture was the emphasis given to the individual, elevating the person to a position of paramount value. This same individualism that is increasingly perceived as a threat to civility in modern culture, documented in such best-selling books as Christopher Lasch's *The Culture of Narcissism* (1979) and

Robert Bellah's *Habits of the Heart* (1986), has its philosophical roots in the Enlightenment; but it has been lavishly reinforced by modern Christianity, including the theory and practice of evangelization. The Enlightenment church was characterized by widespread nominalism and apathy, and it was understandable that revival preaching emphasized the necessity for individual conversion and commitment. But the conjunction of Enlightenment anthropology and revival preaching that emphasized the *individual* — without relating this to society/church — undermined the meaning of church. This lopsided emphasis on the individual has marked evangelical theology right up to the present.

The stereotypical view of evangelization that we have been describing has had far-reaching implications for both message and method. It had a reductionist effect on both. The gospel could be reduced to information that was to be conveyed in what was perceived to be the most efficient way possible. The key problem to be solved was to find the right methods and techniques and to organize a campaign, crusade, or drive. This put a premium on program rather than the formation of a community of disciples.

Western culture has had a long fascination with technology and its problem-solving potential. An oft-quoted truism has it that "if it doesn't have a solution it isn't a problem." A strongly held cultural value is that there is an appropriate technology for every process. These techniques and methods are, of course, furnished by a technocratic culture. Evangelization has been conceptualized and defined largely in terms of these cultural assumptions. If this assertion is true, evangelization itself has been secularized in the sense that it has become a program to be executed according to a certain predetermined formula or it is regarded as merchandise to be marketed. By contrast, the apostle Paul refused to be classed as a "huckster" of the gospel (2 Cor. 2:17).

Sociologists have pointed out that modern society, especially in the way the means of production are organized into ever greater degrees of specialization of function, evolves toward compartmentalization of life for the individual and to *"anonymous social relations"* (Berger, Berger, and Kellner 1973:31). As this process progresses, the "self is now experienced in a partial and segmented way" (:32; also Bibby 1987). The modern self has deeply internalized this alienation.[3] Life must be endured as an existence marked by alienation rather than enjoyed as an integrated whole. *What assurance do we have that secularized modes of evangelization are not sources of alienation rather than means to personal and social reconciliation?* This is a matter of utmost importance.

The gospel is that humankind can be reconciled to God through the mediation of Jesus Christ. Each one is treated with utmost dignity. God calls and invites all people with tenderness and compassion because they are created in the *imago Dei*. But the effect of *technique* is the opposite. It depersonalizes; it separates into parts, resulting in fragmentation. Evangelization that is reduced to efficient techniques and methods becomes a parody of the gospel of reconciliation.

Another issue deserves to be cited and that is the assumption that the modern Western church truly *knows* its culture. It would be more accurate to say the church takes its culture for granted. The fact that the church has for so long been defined by the social classes in which it was embedded indicates that, far from having a critical knowledge of its culture, the church speaks largely with the accent and idiom of the class(es) with which it is identified. The church of Christendom never has been able to shake off its image of being implicated in the power structures of society. The masses believed that they had to look elsewhere for succor. In spite of the great changes in modern society, especially the intermingling of many cultures in all metropolitan areas, there is little evidence that our approach to evangelization, dominated as it has been by technique, has achieved the necessary critical distance from modern culture.

Historical Notes on Evangelization

Evangelization has been a contentious issue both within the church and without. Volumes could be written on the ecclesiastical obstacles would-be evangelists had to face, especially in the seventeenth and eighteenth centuries as they set about their work. The key barrier, but one that the established churches guarded jealously, was the parochial system that required the licensing of each priest or pastor for a specific parish and the conduct of worship only in consecrated sanctuaries. Evangelists always found these restrictions inconvenient and insisted on ranging across such boundaries. Many of them attracted such large crowds that no consecrated place of worship could accommodate the throngs, so they resorted to preaching out-of-doors. This inclination to run roughshod over church law had the effect of loosening the grip of the ecclesiastical system; it had the positive effect of opening the way for evangelization.

The Pietist-Evangelical movement played an important role in reviving the churches at various times. As Hendrik Kraemer (1958:27) observed, "The institutional non-Roman Churches in the second half of the 17th century and the first half of the 18th century had either solidified themselves in a safe orthodoxy (Continent of Europe) or had gone to sleep in a comfortable latitudinarianism." It was this scholastic orthodoxy that produced considered theoretical and theological opposition to mission to the world. Both the Pietist movement and the Evangelical Revival inculcated an activism that directly counteracted this staid orthodoxy. The quickening of spiritual life in the churches became the seedbed for considerable innovation in both social ministries at home and the missionary movement abroad.

Revivalism has had an important leavening effect on the church in critical areas. First and foremost, it has created opportunities for laypeople for Christian service. Kraemer has pointed to the role laypeople played through the modern period in challenging the ecclesiastical establishment and proposing innovations. The most famous evangelist in the latter half of the nineteenth century, Dwight L. Moody, was a layman. If this, in some sense, represents the coming of age of the laity in the church, it must be recalled that it was a long and arduous journey from Justinian von Weltz's failed effort in the seventeenth century to get the German church to endorse missions to Moody's career as evangelist. Revivalism's second contribution was to encourage ecumenical cooperation. From the time of Whitefield and Wesley, revivalism could not be contained by ecclesiastical boundaries. This posed grave problems for the churches that wanted to maintain control over their members. The evangelists were not slow to modernize their methodology. Finney, Moody, and other evangelists skillfully adopted modern technique to augment their ministry (with the problematic results noted above).

Repeatedly, the historian comes to the conclusion that what Christendom has called "evangelism" has made little impact outside the church. Stephen Neill pointed out that evangelists in the nineteenth century, such as D. L. Moody and R. A. Torrey, could assume that their audiences had a certain amount of biblical information and familiarity with the church. Their main task was to elicit personal response and lead people to make a commitment. But it is unwise to operate on such an assumption today. Writing in 1957, Neill cited the Billy Graham Crusades — then in their first flush of success — as his example. Respectful toward Graham and appreciative of his ministry, Neill notes that the vast majority of those who attended and responded at Graham's crusades were people who already had some connection with the church and the gospel. As one who cared deeply about reaching the masses who had never been introduced to Christian faith, Neill (1957:103) insisted that Graham's message and method could not be the answer to reaching people who have no personal acquaintance with the church or things Christian. It was a message for the insider communicated in "church" language.

Evangelistic techniques and methods have multiplied rapidly in the twentieth century. Echoing the conclusion reached by Stephen Neill, Milton Rudnick (1984:199) asserts: "Although people are won for Christ by deliberate, carefully-planned evangelism efforts, the number is not large." The great majority of people who affiliate with a church in the United States do so as a result of a personal relationship. Evangelistic crusades make the public aware of Christian activity, but "the vast majority of those who attend crusades are committed and practicing Christians for whom it is an experience in spiritual uplift" (:202). Similarly, although Christian broadcasting has become a major industry using both radio and television, the scandals in recent years involving certain televangelists have discredited these more public and highly visible so-called evangelistic efforts.

Two Modern Evangelists

We are familiar with the professional evangelist, but there are others who also fill this role and exert wide influence. These brief sketches of two unconventional evangelists of the twentieth century afford an opportunity to observe how contrasting approaches to culture shape the Christian message.

Norman Vincent Peale (1898–1994), one of the best-known religious figures in the United States for a generation, was pastor of the historic Marble Collegiate Church in New York City, 1932–1984. Peale's national reputation derived from the religious empire he built through his popularization of the gospel of positive thinking. Positive thinking has its roots in nineteenth-century American culture, but it had remained on the margins of religious life. Peale skillfully blended liberal theology, orthodox theology, and positive thinking into an amalgam that was "non-creedal, syncretic, and pragmatic" (George 1993:7). Peale got his vocabulary from the mainstream Christian tradition — God, sin, salvation — but promoted an evangelical style and conservative political agenda that gave it emotional appeal among the "middlebrow" classes. He was the great populist preacher who knew his audience. "Animated, humorous, informal, he became an *evangelist* to the new age" (:61). Although he frequently was criticized by other church leaders and theologians, Peale did not bend to criticism. He regarded the middle class his constituency and played to them rather than the intellectuals.

There is no doubt that Peale was closely attuned to changing American culture. He contributed in no small way to the "self help" movement that has burgeoned in American society during the past fifty years. These self-help programs purport to draw on energies hidden within each human being. Peale's key idea was the "belief that through the mind and the subconscious, utilizing techniques of positive thinking and affirmative prayer, one can achieve spiritual harmony and personal power" (:9). In his sermons Peale "developed the theme of the transformative power of personal religion by reiterating three basic themes . . . health, personal achievement or success, and the value of experiential rather than formal religion" (:227). This formula, with its emphasis on the individual, resonated well with the cultural mood. Always the pragmatist, "Peale experimented with whatever 'new measures' came to his attention to recruit new members" (:56). Raised a Methodist with deep roots in the Revival tradition, "Peale called himself an evangelist and compared his preaching style, with its implicit call for conversion, to what old-time revivalists called 'drawing in the net,'" reports Carol V. R. George (:88). More often he referred to himself as "God's salesman."

Was Peale's message a secular gospel or, as he contended, the word of salvation to the masses who comprised his audience? Peale's gospel was "part motivational theory, part mystical pietism, and part primal myth" (:8). Skillful communicator that he was, he held his critics at bay while commanding a large following among business professionals and women. Rather than being a critic of modern culture, Peale was a polished purveyor of a conservative sociopolitical agenda and religious message that fortified the status quo.

In almost every way, C. S. Lewis (1898–1963) presents a contrast with Norman Vincent Peale. Lewis was the unabashed intellectual and university don who converted to Christian faith at age thirty-three. Although seldom called an evangelist, through his many writings and broadcasting Lewis became a major apologist for the Christian faith in the twentieth century. Lewis did not hesitate to call his writings evangelistic, however. In an article in *The Christian Century* in which he defended his writings against the strictures of Norman Pittenger, Lewis (1958:1360) said: "Most of my books are evangelistic, addressed to *tous exo*.... He judges my books *in vacuo* with no consideration of the audience to whom they were addressed or the prevalent errors they were trying to combat." Lewis aimed to fill a need theologians considered beneath their dignity. "When I began," he asserted, "Christianity came before the great mass of my unbelieving fellow-countrymen either in the highly emotional form offered by revivalists or in the unintelligible language of highly cultured clergymen. Most men were reached by neither. My task was therefore simply that of a *translator* ... into the vernacular, into language that unscholarly people would attend to and could understand" (ibid.). Lewis ends his rejoinder saying that his writing would have been quite unnecessary had "real theologians" long ago begun doing the work of "translation" instead of losing touch with common people.

Lewis succeeded in reaching an impressive cross-section of the English-speaking world. He combined several important ingredients. He had the gift of spiritual discern-

ment that enabled him to have a clear sense of the "princi-
palities and powers" that hold the world in their grip. Lewis
spoke compellingly of what faith in God meant in light of
these malignant forces. With great imagination he used his
intellectual powers and academic training to communicate
a message that spoke to a wide range of people about the
inadequacies of the modern worldview. He did not hesitate to draw on his personal biography to narrate the larger
story of faith. In contrast to Norman Vincent Peale, Lewis
consciously spoke across-the-grain of culture with the remarkable result that his readers heard the challenge of the
Christian gospel in fresh terms.

Evangelization and Theology

The evangelist and the theologian have never enjoyed an
easy relationship in modern times. The Jonathan Edwardses
of this world, who combine both vocations in one person,
are a rare species indeed. Theologians have seldom taken
popular evangelists seriously, and evangelists generally do
not get their cues from theologians. The church has been
ill-served by this antagonistic relationship (Pickard 1993). It
is clear that both evangelists and theologians must be concerned to understand the culture in which they live through
the plausibility structure of the reign of God if the work of
either is to have real meaning (Abraham 1989:chap. 9).

The forces of modernity have contributed directly to the
breakup of Christendom. Religion has not been viewed as
a desirable ally of modern culture and has been discredited
by the secularists. From the beginning of the modern period the church was put on the defensive by its critics. This
defensive mood may help account for the fact that theolo-

gians have devoted the bulk of their efforts to reworking
and reinterpreting the Christian tradition to be culturally
acceptable rather than the constructive task of engaging culture in light of the gospel.[4] Consequently, the missional task
has been neglected.

Theologians who uncritically accommodate themselves
to culture forfeit credibility, and those who reject culture
are treated as reactionaries. In the first case, the theologian
offers only an echo of what the culture is saying; in the
other case, by failing to learn to communicate idiomatically,
the theologian is incomprehensible. The theological task is
always to penetrate as deeply as possible into the great existential question that hangs over a culture. At the same time,
a parallel movement must be made into God's Word, si-
multaneously eternal and contemporary, if this generation
is to grasp the way in which the biblical message speaks
salvifically to this audience in the light of the forces that
threaten life.

What we have just said about the theologian may be applied equally to the evangelist. Just as the Old Testament is
careful to distinguish true from false prophets, the possibility of there being false, as well as true, evangelists is always
present. The true evangelist, in the manner of Jesus, de-
clares the truth about the human condition, the world, and
God's way.

The task of the evangelist is a demanding one. To be
credible, evangelization must engage a culture intellectually,
socially, politically, and personally or experientially. Modern culture has its own particular profile in each of these
areas, and these realms impinge on life. To live in modern
urban culture is to be subject to an intellectual climate that
prizes skepticism over certainty and doubt rather than faith.

Large questions having to do with the meaning of human existence and relationships hang in the balance.

Modern culture has become progressively uncertain in its understanding of human society in light of the supreme value given the individual. Ironically, the elevation of the self has not led to greater personal security. On the contrary, modern people seem absorbed in deepening doubts about "self," so we are now bombarded with calls to build self-esteem. Modern consciousness has been shaped by the forces of scientific technology and industrial organization that tear at relationships. To understand what the gospel can mean to people whose lives are divided among many loyalties is a daunting but challenging and essential task. From the outset one knows that to be converted from subservience to the idols of our age may well start at a particular moment, but it will entail a long process of many other conversions.

All of this suggests the importance of the evangelistic task to be supported by theology. Theology that is worked out as a community-building response to the contemporary situation will be lifegiving.

Evangelization and Integrity

The more fully the church embraces the evangelizing task, the more wholly will it realize its integrity. The church cannot sustain its own conviction for the gospel only on the basis of history. The world will not feel challenged by a body that is nostalgic for a time now gone. The church's own experience of the gospel gains vitality in direct proportion to its engagement in witness now. At no point is the power of the gospel made more evident than when men and women cross over the line between the kingdom of this world and the kingdom of God. This move is costly and requires great courage, for God leads the penitent through a reorientation (*metanoia*) and restructuring that touches all dimensions of life: intellectual, social, political, economic, personal, and experiential.

Evangelization and the integrity of the church are inextricably linked. Karl Barth (1962:874) rightly insisted that "a Church which is not as such an evangelizing Church is either not yet or no longer the Church, or only a dead Church, itself standing in supreme need of renewal by evangelization." The test of the church's integrity is whether it is living by the fullness of the gospel and, therefore, witnessing to the gospel's power (Rom. 1:16).

The integrity of the church in the West is under siege because of the extent to which institutionalism has overtaken the church. There are observable signs of this condition. One is the sheer proliferation of programs and activities. Driven by the advice of consultants who tell churches that they must cater to the needs of their publics, churches are operating a veritable supermarket of specialized services to meet the whims and demands of a consumer society. Not to do so is to lose out in the competition for a growing membership. (If Jesus were engaged as consultant for a one-day seminar on evangelization and church development, what would the focal issue be? Does anyone seriously believe that competitive growth is the vision Jesus had for his Body?)

This trivialization of the church through preoccupation with activities is like a cancer that destroys the vitality of the body from within. On the surface the church appears to be alive and well. Inside, there is another condition. The church is largely engaged in recycling the saints rather than proclaiming the good news of the reign of God to the sick, blind, and oppressed in modern culture. Our activist culture has gulled us into mistaking activity for spiritual power and focus. This is an important facet of the cultural captivity into which the church has fallen.

This recalls for us the stinging criticism Roland Allen made eight decades ago of the missionary enterprise.[5] He charged missions with being so preoccupied and encumbered with programs and activities that they were unable to sense the movement of the Holy Spirit. It is significant that only the Pentecostal movement, then in its infancy, heard Allen's message and took it to heart. The Pentecostal movement is the nearest thing we have to a reformation movement in the twentieth century. Rejected by their churches, Pentecostal leaders struck out on their own. They went to the marginal peoples of society and developed the church from the ground up. What effectiveness the church has had among the masses of modern culture has come largely from the Pentecostals, the Salvation Army, and such groups. Now two generations later one sees signs that the Pentecostal-Charismatic movement has increasingly made its peace with modern culture, too, as it has gained in respectability. The church has great difficulty reconciling the demands of integration into respectable social status and the countercultural thrust of Jesus (Luke 4:16–19), for in choosing respectability it begins bartering away its integrity.

A second sign of institutionalism is the proportion of resources that the typical congregation expends on itself as compared to what it contributes to ministry to others. The church in the West, at this moment in history, mirrors the wider culture in turning toward self-preoccupation and away from the world community. The culture reassures us that we need to seek our own interests, but it gives us no clue as to how we may distinguish between necessary stewardship of ourselves and outright selfishness. Our culture rejects the strong medicine of Jesus, who in his first discourse on mission said to his disciples: "Those who find their life will lose it, and those who lose their life for my sake will find it" (Matt. 10:39). We have convinced ourselves that it is by taking care of our "needs" first that we are then prepared to enter into the burdens of others.

This is to suggest, then, that the church in modern culture lacks integrity. It has been bought off by many "good things," but these have distracted the church from its primary task — announcing and demonstrating the reign of God. The way to regain integrity is to return to the evangelizing task. This will require that we break free from the Christendom mentality, on the one hand, and captivity to modern culture, on the other, for that kind of church has effectively been neutered. The power of the reign of God cannot flow through it, and it offers no challenge to the kingdom of the world. It guarantees that the church will be relating only to those who already have, or did have, a connection with the church. Further, it means the church will continue to rely on a vocabulary that is foreign to the masses who for generations have worshiped at other shrines. Finally, it will continue to dull our capacity to hear and respond to the pain and cries of those in our culture who long for liberation through God's gracious saving power.[6]

To put the argument positively, the church of modern culture can be freed from the spreading malaise only by reclaiming the evangelizing task. To reclaim evangelization, however, we must recognize the way we have been taken captive by modern culture, whereby we have been coopted and muffled by the culture. So long as the world can get the church to speak a worldly message in the guise of being religious, the world wins. Jesus claimed that he had "overcome the world." He did that by announcing and living out God's reign. And that is the commission he handed on to his church.

4

Church

In 1975 I visited a friend who was serving as pastor of a new congregation in a suburb of one of Europe's major cities. At that moment he and his wife were trying to help a young woman with a tragic story. Six months before, her boyfriend had taken her to the capital city of the neighboring country and put her to work as a prostitute. Just recently he had brought her back, only to be arrested himself and put in prison for criminal activity. Betina was now pregnant and had neither a home of her own nor family to turn to. At this point she had come into contact with the church. For the first time in her life this sad-eyed young woman encountered people who did not try to exploit her; she was attracted by this congregation, which accepted her in spite of her background. And yet my friend faced a tough dilemma. He said, "If Betina is to find salvation she must have a family. Quite simply, our congregation would have to become her family. She knows no other way to function in society than to be used by others. Unless we give her shelter until she learns to fend for herself, she will continue to be at the mercy of exploitative forces and Betina will not be saved." Then he added ruefully, "But our congregation is too conventional to be able to adapt itself to Betina's needs."

This vignette is a haunting parable of the "conventional" church in modern culture. It puts a spotlight on the local church situated amid awful human tragedy yet lacking the courage and will to become a "saving presence." The local church, of course, has to contend with a complex and sophisticated culture. Unless the church engages this culture by penetrating to the presuppositions on which it rests and out of which it operates, the church's witness will be a sham.

In the 1970s two incisive articles by W. A. Visser 't Hooft (1974; 1977), founding general secretary of the World Council of Churches, in the *International Review of Mission* caught my attention. Visser 't Hooft urged the church to prepare for evangelization in Europe by getting in touch with the growing neo-pagan phenomenon. He challenged us to recognize that "we are now in a situation in which for many Europeans, especially the younger ones, a meeting with the Gospel comes as a new discovery.... Let us hope that in a Europe that has become mission territory, the churches may become in the best sense 'younger' churches" (1977:360). Visser 't Hooft's writings had an unmistakable ring of urgency to them.

Eager to know whether Visser 't Hooft might have given further attention to this concern, I corresponded with him in 1981. I wrote that "I have been wrestling with the relationship between evangelistic message and the condition of Western civilization.... What studies are you aware of which ought to be taken into account as we pursue this question?" Visser 't Hooft replied promptly: "It is not easy to give a short answer to your important question. If I were 10 years younger, I would try to write a book about it. Now

I can only give the outline of such a book. I agree strongly that this is the main issue to which evangelists and missiologists should turn." He attached an outline organized under three heads: (1) Historical, (2) Battlefields, and (3) The Antipagan Witness.

In the first part Visser 't Hooft called for an analysis of the "anti-Christian and pagan elements in Western civilization." He was convinced the churches had been misled by their uncritical acceptance of the myth of a Christian West versus "a pagan rest of the world." In part two, Visser 't Hooft had his eye on three battlefields: literature, sex, and the counterculture of the younger generation. Under the third head — the antipagan witness — he proposed a fivefold response to neo-paganism (reproduced here in full):

1. Over against syncretism and indifferentism, the clear affirmation that God was in Christ and that Christ is the Saviour whose name is to be proclaimed to all men.

2. Over against the pantheism in much paganism, the affirmation that God is not an "it" but a "Thou."

3. Over against the vitalism which considers biological life holy, the affirmation that it is "Zoe," not "Bios," which is the true life.

4. Over against the egocentricity of paganism, the biblical conception of the I-Thou relation as central.

5. Over against sex as self-expression, the sexual relation as a covenant. Monogamy [is] not a "moral" issue but a gift of God.[1]

This was the kind of homework that Visser 't Hooft was recommending to the churches in the West. He lamented that few theologians and pastors were paying attention to such issues. "What courses concerning neo-paganism," he asked, "are given in our theological faculties and in our lay training institutes?" (1977:360). In the face of evident spiritual hunger and human need, the churches were guilty of turning a deaf ear to their world. No wonder the world no longer took the church seriously.

The times were out of joint, violence stalked the land, and people felt hopeless. In this situation word came to Habakkuk: "Write the vision; make it plain.... For there is still a vision for the appointed time" (Hab. 2:2b–3a). Philosophers and poets have long described modern culture as being in decline. At the end of the twentieth century, the modern project is widely regarded as being in the grips of enervating crisis. Furthermore, the church is perceived as participating in this crisis. Against this view, we are arguing for a threefold vision. In times of crisis, hope is rekindled by turning to God and the *missio Dei*. It is from this that we gain clear perspective on the world and God's commitment to the world. But this perspective gains in power only when it is attuned to the "appointed time," or God's *kairos*. It means that we must read our times through God's eyes and respond out of God's passion for the world. Otherwise we will be engulfed in the prevailing despair. The third dimension is confidence that the people of God can be renewed in their covenantal relationship and mission. The only resource the church has that distinguishes it from all other movements or groups is the gospel. A renewed church will be a church with integrity and a clear vision of its missional responsibility to its own culture.

What Is the Church?

The church emerged in response to the work of Jesus the Messiah as the community committed to his lordship. Significantly, the New Testament leaves a series of questions about the church unanswered: When precisely did the church begin? Is the church *sui generis*, or does it have historical and theological antecedents? If so, what are they? Why was the matter of polity left so ambiguous? Nowhere does the New Testament give a precise definition of the church (Schnackenburg 1965:9–54; Barth 1962:683).[2] Rather, what we find is a plethora of images and metaphors, none of which alone is sufficient to convey the full meaning of "church." Already within the first generation tension began to build between the mode of church that emphasized *being* rather than *function*, and *institution* over *movement* (Käsemann 1964:chap. 3; Küng 1967:179–91). It is evident that the definition or starting point adopted will determine the outcome.

Old Testament Roots

One of the most significant pivots in the biblical narrative is the election of Abraham. With great economy Genesis 12:1–3 records God's action establishing a covenant with Abraham, and he becomes the archetype of the "people of God."[3] God is the initiator and guarantor of this covenanted relationship. The covenant structured and defined the responsibility it entailed for the people of God.

As the people whose identity is derived from this covenant, a peoplehood has been conferred on Abraham and his descendants that marks them off from all other nations and peoples: *They are now responsible both to God and to the nations.* God exhorted the people: "I am the LORD your God; sanctify yourselves therefore, and be holy, for I am holy" (Lev. 11:44). It is this sanctified character that qualifies God's people to represent God and serve the nations on God's behalf. Whenever the people of Israel violate the covenant by joining their neighbors in worship of the gods, they forsake their true character and defame God before the world. They have turned their back on God and joined the peoples in rebellion against the Lord.

The special vocation of the people of God is to enter into vital, redemptive relationship with all peoples. This they can do only out of the resource of their God-given identity as the Holy Nation. The people of God have been given an unconventional nationality precisely to enable them to maintain their identity as a set-apart-people for the service to the peoples. Therefore, their identity dare not be defined in ethnic terms but as moral and spiritual. The covenant thus is the vehicle through which God is extending the divine "blessing" of salvation to all the nations. Because God's covenant is universal in scope, all other ethnic or national identities are relativized. The covenant people are characterized by an unshakable allegiance to God and service to the nations. This service takes the form of being mediators and reconcilers between God and the nations. The Abrahamic covenant, which is reiterated four times in Genesis, emphasizes the instrumental character of the identity of the people of God.[4] They are defined by their mission or task. God promises blessing to Israel, but it is linked to their service to the nations. God blesses Israel through the praise they win from the nations.

This covenantal form is maintained in the New Testament. The apostle Paul interprets his mission and that of the church in essentially the same terms. After speaking about how he became a servant "according to the gift of God's grace," Paul describes the role of the church: "that through the church the wisdom of God in its rich variety might now be made known" (Eph. 3:7, 10). As a practical, rather than a philosophical or speculative theologian, Paul understands the church to be directly involved in the work of reconciling the world to God (cf. 2 Cor. 5:11–21) [M. Barth 1974:1:363–65].

The Jewish philosopher and biblical scholar Martin Buber (1950:10) characterized the Christian faith incisively in these words: "Christianity *begins* [*sic*] as diaspora and mission. The mission means in this case not just diffusion; it is the life-breath of the community and accordingly the basis of the new People of God." This definition faithfully reflects the thrust of the Abrahamic covenant and resonates strongly with the apostle Paul's self-understanding.

Each of these three statements is structured around a tripartite relationship: God, people of God/church, the nations/world. The covenant appoints the people of God to a mediatory role. To be sure, the people of God have repeatedly reneged on their covenantal responsibility by collapsing the difference between themselves and the culture. Covenant renewal always meant that the people returned to their vocation of standing between God and the world as servants.

New Testament Development

Jesus was not at pains to define the church. Instead he called it into being in a new act of covenant making. The Abra-

hamic covenant is the prototype for the reconstituted people
of God. This point is made with particular effect in the
letter to the Hebrews (1:1–3; 2; 3:1–6; 6; 8).

During the last supper Jesus interpreted his work to the
disciples using the language of covenant. He lifted out three
dimensions. First, as they ate together, Jesus instituted the
Lord's Supper in recognition of "the new covenant in my
blood" (Luke 22:20; cf. 1 Cor. 11:25), God's order of salvation. The "new" covenant bears striking similarities with
the old, but through the work of the perfect mediator, Jesus
Christ, God has transformed or remade it. Second, it was
to be a covenant of service (Luke 22:24–27). This immediately places it at odds with the conventions of the world,
where it is taken for granted that "the kings of the Gentiles
lord it over them." Indeed, the moving christological hymn
given in Philippians 2:1–11 interprets Jesus' Messiahship in
terms of this covenant of service wherein redemptive power
is defined as self-giving love. After the resurrection, Jesus
adds the third dimension, namely, that this covenant is in
behalf of all "nations" (Luke 24:46–48).

Jesus and the New Testament writers pass silently over
the question of how the church is to be organized. The
New Testament records only a few decisions taken in response to specific situations, such as the appointing of
deacons in the first days of the church (Acts 6:1–6). Instead, the focus is kept on the real story line — how the
gospel about God's decisive action in Jesus Christ was being shared with growing circles of people, and the response
they were making to it.

Structures per se are timebound. Invariably structures
undergo change in response to the environment, which
itself is continually changing. Those that do not prove flex-

ible and adaptable are soon regarded as obsolete and must be discarded. But the process is never easy. Enormous resources can be used up in defending and preserving archaic structures. The church, like all human enterprises, readily looks to its structures to ensure the continuity of the faith. But the New Testament emphasizes the fundamental identity and purpose of the church as the people of God. This peoplehood is what the Holy Spirit uses to give life and move the church forward. The church cannot exist without institutional arrangements, but it is the Spirit alone who gives the people of God life and renews them in their identity and purpose.

Historical Reality of the Church

An important fact about the church in modern Western culture is that the church has been a part of this culture for a millennium and a half. The place of the church in Western culture has undergone many changes throughout this long period. With regard to status and influence in society, many perceive the church to have been progressively marginalized over the past three hundred years. At the moment we are not debating whether this is a positive or negative development. We only note that the church's position in culture has changed markedly. In light of this trend, how should we think about the future of the church in modern culture?

In reflecting on this long history, several summary observations may help focus important issues. First, we must acknowledge that what has passed as "Christian" culture was largely myth, a fiction used to give legitimacy to an elaborate religio-political system (Delumeau 1977). This is not to overlook the enormous contribution Christians have made to Western and modern culture. Rather, it is to remind us that the reality was far more complex and ambiguous than the standard rendering.

The second observation has to do with the role of coercion in gaining and sustaining the church's position of power prior to the modern period. Like the people of Israel, the church has frequently chosen to join the Philistines, assuming a *persona* that was not that of "the new covenant in my blood." The antagonism that many among the masses of the modern period feel toward the church is rooted in historical experience. Charlemagne's "Christianization" of the Saxons, the Crusades, the sale of indulgences, and the Inquisition have all stained the collective memory. Coercion, which was foundational to Christendom, perverted and mocked the gospel, and the seeds sown have produced a harvest of cynical disdain for Christianity still in evidence in the twentieth century.

Third, the church of Christendom gave up its evangelical sense of mission to its culture as it became fully acculturated and domesticated. Evangelical mission cannot be conceived of except in terms of covenantal relationship with the Triune God, and this involves the question of where primary allegiance is given. Without mission the church becomes something other than what it was called to be. Whenever the church takes its identity from its sociohistorical context, rather than its covenant with God, it loses its distinctive vocation.

Mission Consciousness

The church lives from the consciousness of its fundamental identity. We have stressed that the ecclesial consciousness to be found in the church of modern culture was bequeathed to it by Christendom, and this is patently nonmissionary. Further, we have argued that there is a direct link between this historical fact and the present lassitude of the church in Western culture. History warns us that reformation is difficult in the extreme. To assume that this fundamental question can be addressed through organizational change is to trivialize the problem. (Organizational structures are indeed important but remain nonetheless secondary.) The true starting place is a renewal of the church in its covenantal relationship to the Triune God. Genuine renewal will engage all dimensions of life: spiritual, theological, intellectual, practical. It will ignite the devotion of God's people to serve God by bearing witness in the world. A vital ecclesial consciousness — that is, an identity based on the church's covenantal relationship to God — always consists of these two missional aspects: the inward and the outward.

Inward Mission Consciousness

We have called for a vision of the church in modern culture that is a church with ecclesial integrity. Such a church is the people of God living out their fundamental purpose, mission. In Emil Brunner's potent aphorism, "The Church exists by mission, just as a fire exists by burning" (1931:108).[5] The fire of mission is God's passion for the world's salvation. When the people of God live in covenantal relationship with God, they will find this fire burning within them, too. This is the true energy of Christian existence. Yet the stance assumed in most theological studies — reflecting the condition of the church itself — is of a nonmissional church. The fire is absent.

In the twentieth century certain scholars have made im-

portant contributions to ecclesiology in the areas of biblical
studies and theology (Berkhof 1979:344; Van Engen 1992:
35ff). Some would agree with Brunner's point that mission is constitutive of the identity of the church. At the
existential level, however, scholars appear to be as diffi-
dent as ever about mission as evidenced by the way they
continue to exclude it from the main body of theological
work. It is no surprise that the secular academy remains
hostile to "confessional" Christian faith. But seminaries
and theological faculties, under the influence of the secular academy, have declined to accept the *missio Dei* as the
organizing principle of the theological curriculum, and it
plays no role in the conceptualization of pastoral formation. If we measure the effects of theological education by
what happens in the congregation, then we would have to
say that twentieth century ecclesiology has done little to
change ecclesial self-understanding. The way congregations
in modern culture allocate their financial resources indicates that ecclesial consciousness is shaped largely by the
agenda of self-maintenance as a community of worship
and pastoral services, a perspective pandered to and reinforced by the emphasis on "marketing the church" (Webster
1992; Shelley and Shelley 1992; Guinness 1993; Kenneson
1993). What are the resources for challenging and changing
the present situation? Three ingredients are essential to the
cultivation of a consciousness of mission.

The Great Commission. One of the gains for the
church, as a result of the modern missionary movement,
has been the recovery of the Great Commission. The Protestant Reformers had interpreted this portion of scripture
as having authority only for the primitive church. After
1800 the Great Commission was accepted as having con-

tinuing validity for the church. However, in our reading of the Great Commission — regarded by many as the charter of the modern mission movement — we have done so, the past two hundred years, through the lenses provided by Christendom. The result has been an emphasis on territory; that is, the territory of heathendom versus the territory of Christendom,[6] on *"going"* as the imperative rather than on *"making disciples,"* mission defined as what happens "out there." Apart from being faulty exegesis, this reading reinforced the traditional view that *mission* did not belong within Christendom.[7]

The church in the West must be freed of this distorted understanding of the Great Commission, a notion shaped by the powerful Christendom reality and reinforced by the way it was interpreted during the colonial era.[8] Indeed, the Great Commission judges this deformation and points the church to missionary faithfulness. Christians in modern Western culture will learn to see their culture in light of God's claim on the world if they grasp the thrust of the Great Commission.

Reading the Great Commission in its biblical context has the potential to radicalize the church's vision of itself in relation to the world, the environment in which the church exists (Arias and Johnson 1992).[9] *The Great Commission is a foundational ecclesiological statement, for it is addressed to the disciple community, not autonomous individuals.* It conjoins ecclesiality and apostolicity. The Great Commission thus sets the basic agenda of the church — making men and women disciples of the reign of God wherever the church is present until the end of time. Discipling men and women involves enabling them to embrace and incarnate the fullness of God's reign in their lives. The training of pastors,

theologians, and missiologists for ministry in modern Western culture ought to be based on a biblical understanding
rather than historical precedents and theological distortions.
Discipleship involves living out the Great Commission.

The urgent task before us is to rethink the function
of the Great Commission biblically and theologically. The
modern mission movement did indeed reclaim and restore
this portion of scripture to the church's awareness, but this
was done without a fundamental rethinking of the nature
of the church as it had been redefined from the fourth century within the matrix of the *corpus Christianum*.[10] Instead,
the Great Commission was understood primarily in terms
of motivating individual Christians to go or to support missions, in the same way appeal has been made countless times
to a text like Isaiah 6:1–8. This inspirational and motivational dimension has indeed been indispensable to the
modern mission movement, but it fails to do justice to the
meaning and function of the text in the canon (Michel
1983; Bosch 1983 and 1991; Legrand 1986; Davies and
Allison 1992).

The Great Commission structures the church's relation
to the world. To put the matter in sociological terms, institutions mediate the relations between an individual or group
and the world. These include such matters as conventions
that regulate social relationships and extend to all realms
where interaction is occurring (Bellah 1991:287–93). The
Great Commission institutionalizes mission as the *raison
d'être*, the controlling norm, of the church. To be a disciple
of Jesus Christ and a member of his body is to live a missionary existence in the world. There is no doubt that this
was how the earliest Christians understood their calling.

Preparing for mission in the region of "Jerusalem, Judea

and Samaria" that comprises our Western culture will require that we approach this frontier in missional rather than pastoral terms.[11] In this respect, the cross-cultural mission preserves for us a basic model of how the church is to relate to the world in all times and places. We assume that the cross-cultural missioner must treat the host culture with sensitivity and respect, starting with learning the language and the various symbol systems that comprise a culture. As modern societies have become increasingly pluralized, this "cross-cultural" perspective becomes ever more imperative for all Christian witness. Ministry always emanates from a particular vantage point, with the disciple serving as ambassador of the kingdom of God to a culture. The motif of the resident alien, found in both Old and New Testaments, is another way of expressing the fact that the church is to be "in but not of the world."

We must come to grips with a culture that is in crisis and transition. At the same time we should become more self-aware of the assumptions that have controlled mission studies and missionary action up to the present. The cross-cultural experience of mission over the past two centuries represents an invaluable resource for the training of missiologists and missionaries to Western culture. Indeed, mission should be conceived of as an inherently cross-cultural action, a movement mandated by the Triune God into territory that does not acknowledge the reign of God. Geography and nationality are entirely secondary concerns.

The Model of Mission. Luke's account of the Acts of the Apostles describes the working out of this missionary existence from the beginning: at his ascension Jesus gives the still disconsolate and disoriented disciples their defining purpose (1:8); forty days later at Pentecost the church is constituted on the basis of that mission (2:41–47); and the remainder of Acts records the unfolding of that mission.[12] In two descriptive passages Luke provides what we may take as the normative twofold model by which the church works out its missionary existence in the world.

Acts 11:19–26 depicts the *organic mode*. Under the impact of fierce persecution in the environs of Jerusalem (6: 8–8:4) the disciple community scattered, with a contingent going to Antioch, at that time the third largest city in the Roman world. Far from being intimidated by the persecution they had endured, the disciples continued their evangelizing activity — the very thing that got them into trouble in Jerusalem — and continued to witness indeterminately both to Jews and Gentiles. The result was that "the hand of the Lord was with them, and a great number became believers and turned to the Lord" (11:21). Luke presents no honor roll of outstanding evangelists. Reading this account in the context of the varied encounters the young community was having, it is evident the disciple communities challenged the regnant plausibility structure of their culture on the basis of the claims of the reign of God (cf. Acts 17:6f). Witness to God's reign, present and coming, was at the heart of the disciple community's life. The church grew organically. This mode has been the main vehicle of the expansion of the church historically and is an authentic outworking of the Great Commission.

Acts 13:1–3 describes a contrasting but complementary mode. The Holy Spirit led the church at Antioch to an innovation. Certain individuals were set apart for an itinerant ministry that would enable the faith to spread to key cities and regions throughout the Roman world. This created the precedent for the *sending mode* and, by extension, cross-cultural mission, which subsequently, played a critical role in the expansion of the church precisely because it set a guard against the parochialism — the entropic syndrome — that is the slow death of the faith. The Great Commission continually holds this dimension before the church.

Luke's account of the development of the early church may be seen as proceeding from the thesis statement in Acts 1:8. The model for mission is the missionary church actualizing its true existence through the two modes (11:19–26 and 13:1–3). From Acts we understand that the Holy Spirit leads the church in working out its obedience to the Great Commission. No place is given for dichotomous thinking — home versus foreign missions. The Antioch church is the base from which both expressions of missionary obedience emanate. The authenticity and vitality of the church in its local environment is validated by the fact that the Holy Spirit calls from it select individuals, with confirming action by the church, to be witnesses to the gospel among Jews and Gentiles farther away and where cultural and linguistic barriers may be greater. But those individuals also feel themselves accountable to the church through which they receive their commission.

The Reign of God as Controlling Criterion. The phrase "kingdom of God" occurs only eight times in Acts (1:3, 6; 8:12; 14:22; 19:8; 20:25; 28:23, 31). This does not mean it is of little importance. Luke reports that Jesus in his final forty days with the disciples was occupied with expounding to them the meaning of the reign of God (1:3). And the last thing we hear of Paul is that he is prisoner in Rome where he "welcomed all who came to him, proclaiming the kingdom of God and teaching about the Lord Jesus Christ" (28:30–31). The emerging Messianic movement is based on the reign of God as its criterion. The Great Commission calls the church to keep the kingdom as its central focus — dethroning idols, freeing people from demonic powers and oppression, healing the sick, and inviting people into saving relationship with God through Jesus the Messiah. The model of mission identified by Luke guides the church in witnessing to and living out the reality of God's reign in the world. Whenever the church lives out of that dynamic, there will be a strong mission consciousness. Conversely, when awareness of the kingdom of God is weak, there will be a corresponding feeble sense of mission or a reliance on missionary approaches motivated by sources other than the reign of God.

Outward Mission Consciousness

The church renewed in its inward mission consciousness in response to the reign of God will also be revitalized in its outward manifestation of mission. We must seek to understand the world, particularly modern Western culture, in missional perspective because it is the object of this extraordinary undertaking. More particularly, it requires that we become self-critically aware of the "kingdom of the Western world," which is counterposed to the reign of God. All cultures are human constructs. None, including the culture of Christendom, approximates the kingdom of God.[13] Consequently, wherever "this gospel of the kingdom of God" is proclaimed, deep tension with the world appears.

Because we are indigenous to this culture, we easily accept the dubious assumption that we know it in its depths. But many Christians have great difficulty distinguishing between God and Caesar, or Mammon, in their loyalties. It remains a scandal to many who have been shaped by the assumptions of Christendom and "Christian culture" that we must subject the fundamental presuppositions on which our culture rests to rigorous missiological scrutiny and criticism. They accept that the individual needs to be saved from personal sin, but this is understood as having to do with one's personal status before God rather than involving our social relations along with the wider culture.

To train Christians of modern culture to adopt a missionary perspective toward their culture will require assuming a countercultural stance. Only a self-conscious standing against the mainstream will enable the disciple to overcome the undertow of resistance, including that of fellow Christians, to raising these fundamental questions concerning our culture. Any critical profile of modern culture would need to include such basic themes as the view of the human being, the importance of technique, and the role of power and violence.

The Modern Self. The crowning achievement of the Enlightenment was the emergence of "the autonomous self." Traditional society had no place for such autonomy. The individual's place was assured by virtue of conformity to the role or station defined by society. The Enlightenment proclaimed freedom for the individual from such arbitrary constraints (Brown 1968:90–106). It was argued that the human being can achieve its fullest potential only if set free. The corollary conviction was the potential of humans to solve all problems through reason.

The ideals of freedom and rationality soon entered political discourse and were enshrined in both the United States Declaration of Independence (1776) with its "self-evident truths" and the French Statement of Human and Civil

Rights (1789). "Life, liberty, and the pursuit of happiness" became hallmarks of modern liberal culture.

Since the eighteenth century, modern culture has regarded the autonomous individual as the ideal for personhood. Positively, this has encouraged people the world over to resist and reject political tyranny and inhumane conditions. A new appreciation of the dignity of the human being and the consequent emphasis on "human rights" are fruits of this movement. But certain other facts are inescapable. Two hundred years after Immanuel Kant defined enlightenment as the "coming of age" of humankind through the throwing off of external constraints, and after vast sociopolitical changes that have greatly enlarged individual freedoms, we are a culture driven by the quest for *self-esteem*, which has proved to be such an elusive goal.

The temptation to "be as God" in modern culture has taken the form of making self the goal. Ironically, enlightenment has fostered alienation (Gunton 1985). Modern culture's love affair with "expressive individualism" is "corrosive of both true love for the self as well as love of others. Conceiving of persons as unrelated and finally unrelatable social 'atoms' allows one to recognize self-seeking and self-expression, but not self-love" (Pope 1993). This has produced far-reaching consequences for inhabitants of modern culture.[14] We can do no more than note several issues. First, it may well be asked whether we now have a sound understanding of personhood at all. Second, our long preoccupation with the "self" has resulted in the atrophying of our sense of what makes for a viable society (Bellah 1991 and 1986). And third, we urgently need to reconsider the meaning of Christian conversion in light of the impact of modern culture on Christian thought and practice by which belief has been separated from ethics.[15]

Technique. Modernity is the culture of scientific technology, a point made with great force decades ago by Jacques Ellul (1967). This means not only that we have developed more and more machines to do our work; it points to the fact that *technique* has been woven into the very fabric of our lives. The ways we communicate and relate to others are shaped by technique. The impact of the modern system on the human being has been the subject of sustained study by social scientists. A central conclusion is that technological culture results in anomie and alienation. The rise of the counterculture movement of the 1960s was, in part, a reaction to this controlling characteristic of modern culture.

Modern technology is displayed at its most brilliant perhaps in the appliances of modern warfare. The United States government force-fed the military-industrial complex over the past fifty years with huge infusions of capital to enable continual technological innovation in order to build the most sophisticated weapons that could be devised. It has been pointed out that the way a nation wages war reflects profoundly its culture. The technological sophistication of the Western military machine is a projection of modern culture. It is salutary to recall, therefore, the failure of the United States military campaign in Southeast Asia in which technological warfare was defeated by a poor peasant army that was fighting for its political, not simply its military, life (Baritz 1985).

If Christian witness is to engage technological culture effectively, important questions must be considered. On the one hand, we must ask whether the church has taken account of the nature of modern technological culture and its impact on the human being — individually and collectively. On the other, the church can ill afford to rely uncritically on *technique* in its witness. If technique leads to alienation, and if the church uncritically allows technique to shape all its ministries, what reason do we have to believe that our witness will not contribute to further alienation rather than reconciliation with God and fellow humans? To ask the question is not to presume to have an answer. But if we want to engage modern culture with the gospel, it is a question we cannot evade.

Power and Violence. Power is central to human existence. Life can be lived only because of power, that is, the means to set goals and work them out. More than we usually recognize, we are all preoccupied with power. The consciousness of power in modern culture has been heightened by the confidence that through scientific technology we actually possess the means to bend the forces of nature to our purposes, control our environment, conquer disease, and be masters of our destiny. These achievements have been real but remain relative and ambiguous at best. More sobering still is the extent to which modern culture is a culture of violence, that is, power turned destructive.

In his Nobel Lecture on Literature, Aleksandr Solzhenitsyn characterized modern culture: "Violence, continually less restrained by the confines of a legality established over the course of many generations, strides brazenly and victoriously through the whole world ... [which] is being flooded with the crude conviction that force can do everything and righteousness and innocence nothing" (1972:28). This should not surprise us when we understand the way the myth of redemptive violence has been used to give legitimacy to so much in modern culture, from children's cartoons to foreign policy (Wink 1992).

In spite of the pretenses and the illusions purveyed by modern culture of mastery over life forces, it is demonstrably incapable of delivering itself from the forces of death. These powers infiltrate every area of human life, perverting and ultimately destroying that which was created good.[16] Only the message of the reign of God, in which power is defined by the cross, holds out hope to the men and women who inhabit modern culture. It is through *metanoia,* a turning toward God's new heaven and new earth, that we have the promise of salvation.

The Future of the Church

In a celebrated series of lectures in 1949 on *Christianity and History,* Herbert Butterfield looked back on fifteen hundred years of Christian history and concluded that Christendom had in fact run out of steam. In his view "we can just about begin to say that at last no man is now a Christian because of government compulsion" or because it will win an individual social or economic benefits. Butterfield was heartened by what he observed. "This fact makes the present day the most important and the most exhilarating period in the history of Christianity for fifteen hundred years.... We are back for the first time in something like the earliest centuries of Christianity, and those early centuries afford some relevant clues to the kind of attitude to adopt" (1949:135). As a historian, Butterfield was under no obligation to offer a blueprint of the church of the future, but brilliant insight is not enough. The intervening forty-five years have brought no significant change of trends in the historic churches of Christendom, while, at the same time, the Christian *ecumene* worldwide has continued to make steady gains in Africa, Asia, and Latin America both in numerical strength and in translating the Christian faith into the many vernaculars. The multiple centers of Christian vitality are to be found largely outside historical Christendom.

The future of Christian witness in modern culture is intimately connected with the shape of the church of the future. The vision we seek is of the church as the worthy instrument of God's passion to redeem the world. Such a church will be a people identifiable because they are a "holy nation" who "proclaim the mighty acts" of God (1 Pet. 2:9). This church has one overriding purpose and that is to be God's ministers of reconciliation in the world (2 Cor. 5:11–21). But how do we move from this ideal to the living situation?

Karl Rahner, one of the leading Christian theologians of the twentieth century, grappled with this question over several decades. Rahner was particularly interested in the form of the church. As a Roman Catholic, he was convinced that the heavily institutionalized ecclesiastical system could not sustain the life of the ordinary Roman Catholic in the future. Rahner took his clues from the early church. And after the Base Ecclesial Communities emerged in Latin America, he drew on their experience. In view of the collapse of historical Christendom, and the consequent change in the character of the church, he described the church of the future as "a little flock." Members of this little flock "will be Christians only because of their own act of faith attained in a difficult struggle and perpetually achieved anew. Everywhere will be diaspora and the diaspora will be everywhere"

(Rahner 1967:78f). So-called Christian nations will have disappeared, and Christians will be a minority. Rahner believed this changed status promises to free the church to take up its missionary task. "The community . . . although a minority . . . stands under order to engage in missionary activity."[17] Indeed, this minority status will turn out to be a genuine advantage in carrying out its witness. For Rahner it was clear that the church of the future would be built from the ground up by base communities that were free to pursue their mission. It is a radical but hopeful vision.

The Rahnerian vision rings true because renewal of the church — as well as renewal of Israel in the Old Testament — starts with renewal of the covenant with the Triune God. This leads to a reclaiming of the church's fundamental identity. Genuine renewal has never come from the culture.[18] On the contrary, true renewal calls the people of God to turn their backs on the cultural idols that have enthralled them in order that they might once again become instruments of God's saving intention for the world.

Notes

Chapter 1: Integrity

1. James Woodforde (1935/1963:485): "March 6 [1795], Friday. Mr. Girling called on me this Morning and paid Me, for Tithe for Mr. Custance for 1794 18. 18. 6. Mr. Custance, Mr. and Mrs. Corbould, and Mr. Stoughton of Sparham, dined & spent the Afternoon with us and stayed till after 9. o'clock at Weston Parsonage. We gave them for Dinner a Couple of boilded Chicken and Pigs Face, very good Peas Soup, a boiled Rump of Beef very fine, a prodigious fine, large and very fat Cock-Turkey rosted, Maccaroni, Batter Custard Pudding with Jelly, Apple Fritters, Tarts and Raspberry Puffs. Desert, baker Apples, nice Nonpareils, brandy Cherries and Filberts. Wines, Port & Sherries, Malt Liquors, Strong Beer, bottled Porter &c. After Coffee and Tea we got to Cards, limited Loo, at 1d. per Counter. . . . All our Dinner was very nicely cooked indeed." The *Diary* contains frequent references to eating and feasting. For the well-off food was cheap, and the household was run by a retinue of servants. Woodforde conducted his clerical duties rather mechanically.

2. E. P. Thompson (1966), chapter 11, "The Transforming Power of the Cross," is a study of the relationship of the Methodist Church to the working class in the nineteenth century. Thompson does not disguise his hostility toward the church.

3. A comprehensive study of this crisis is that by Dutch historian, Jan Romein (1978). He concludes chapter 32, "Babel and Bible," as follows: "The religious crisis at the turn of the century produced two failures. The first, the failure of modernism, led to a permanent decline of faith in the absolute authority of the churches;

the second, the failure of the churches to identify itself with the social reform movement, has, on the contrary, helped it to remain an
important social factor to this day" (p. 493).

4. Karl Barth (1972:426): Commenting on Romans 12:1 —
"This is the meaning of the words: — *I beseech you therefore, brethren.*
Break off — all ye who follow my thoughts, worship with me, and
are pilgrims with me — break off your thinking that it may be a
thinking of God; break off your dialectic, that it may be indeed dialectic; break off your knowledge of God, that it may be what, in
fact, it is, the wholesome disturbance and interruption which God in
Christ prepares, in order that He may call men home to the peace
of His Kingdom."

5. This section draws on the review article by Pierre Renard
(1986:350–54). See further, Maurice Vidal (1989:225–37). Cardinal
Suhard incurred criticism for what appeared to be less than decisive
leadership during the years of the Vichy government. However, no
such doubts have been raised about his passion for evangelizing and
shepherding the masses.

6. Cited by Bryan Green (1951:2). In his pastoral letter
"Growth or Decline?" Suhard (1953:123, 147) discussed "The Loss
of the Masses" and stated that "the methods necessary for the re-
Christianization of the world are as different as they possibly can be
from those that were traditional in the ages of 'Christendom.'"

7. Cited by F. H. Littell (1979:18–30). Karl Barth (1959:64)
refers to this statement by "General Superintendent Günter Jacob
in Cottbus" in his "Letter to a Pastor in the German Democratic
Republic." Although demurring at making such a historical judgment, Barth agrees that "it is certain that something resembling this
approaching end begins to show itself dimly everywhere."

8. J. C. Hoekendijk (1966:134–37) introduced this term into
the World Council of Churches discussion of "the missionary structure of the congregation" in the 1960s, a term he gleaned from "some
recent literature."

Chapter 2: Mission

1. Darrell L. Guder has brought to my attention documents
such as Charlemagne's *Admonitio generalis* of 789, chapter 82, that

instructs the pastors "to preach those things which are just and right and lead to eternal life." This points to the genuine pastoral concern that continued to be present in the church of Christendom and that helped mitigate the excesses and abuses that people experienced at other points, thus balancing out the picture.

2. The Brazilian Catholic theologian Leonardo Boff, in a study of Luther as reformer, paints a graphic picture of conditions in sixteenth-century Europe: "In semifeudal and mercantilist Europe of the fifteenth and sixteenth centuries, the church was a fundamental part of the structure. The Roman See and the bishops, especially in Germany, had great economic, political, juridical and military interests. It should not be forgotten that the Pope had great temporal power with innumerable treaties and benefits. In the semifeudal and mercantile bourgeois order, there existed relations of vassals and subjects, lords and servants, colonizers and colonized. More concretely, religious persuasion as well as armed coercion were used to keep the peasants in submission, despite frequent uprisings in Bohemia, Swabia, France and other parts of central Europe. The feudal aristocracy and the mercantilist bourgeois society worked out a pact with the clergy (who also had secular power) so that the church became the central factor in the reproduction of the semifeudal and mercantilist society. Thus the church, in its multi-functional nature, consecrated and solidified the relations of the *status quo,* which were relations of domination" ("Lutero entre la reforma y la liberación," *Revista Latinoamericana de Teología* [Jan.–April 1984]:92. Translated and cited by Richard Shaull [1991:27].)

3. Except for the sixteenth-century Anabaptists (Yoder 1984). There were continuing currents of reform, of course, such as that of the Puritans in England, which sought to bring renewal among both clergy and laity (Collinson 1967:159–76). My thanks to Leslie P. Fairfield for providing this citation.

4. This characterization is made of the official ecclesiastical stance. It should be noted, however, that during the eighteenth and nineteenth centuries various initiatives were taken, many without formal sanction of the church, as a direct response to the urgent social needs among the working classes. In the British Isles, the Evangelical Revival had a leavening effect that resulted in the for-

mation of a range of voluntary societies. In Germany the impressive diaconal movement sprang up. In a personal communication, Darrell L. Guder indicates that "much of what later became Germany's social welfare system from Bismarck onwards was prepared here." Another manifestation of this Christian responsiveness to society was represented in a movement such as that of the Blumhardt family. Germany also had the Innere Mission movement, which combined evangelistic and philanthropic ministries. Edward Pfeiffer (1908:chap. 22) discusses "Inner Mission Work." He reports that "the adoption of the term 'die Innere Mission,' was suggested by the nature of the work proposed, namely, the reformation and moral and spiritual renewal of the national church itself, 'die Volkskirche,' which had lapsed into an alarming condition of degeneracy. The idea was to arouse the believers, the living members of the state church to a sense of the dire extremity of the nominal Christendom about them, which had become a virtual heathendom" (:290).

5. Berkhof (1964:32–34 and 1979:411) surveys and summarizes ecclesiological studies from the nineteenth century. He discusses the wholesale neglect of mission by theologians and notes that Karl Barth is the exception. However, Barth's own work in this regard has yet to be acknowledged.

6. The definitive and comprehensive account of the development of mission studies remains with Olav G. Myklebust (1957).

7. Gustav Warneck, "The Mutual Relations of Evangelical Missionary Societies," in James Johnston, ed. (1888:2:431–37) criticized Anglo-American attitudes and more especially the fact that some British Methodists were engaged in missionary work in Berlin at that time. John Paul II's Papal Encyclical, *Redemptoris Missio,* December 7, 1990, favors maintaining this distinction. See paragraphs 32, 33, 34. The Pope has called for a "reevangelization" of lapsed "Christian societies."

8. Even this slogan is shadowed by the Christendom legacy. It can be read as meaning that "missionary structure" is only one of several options and not necessarily the primary one. Some advocated a rephrasing so as to make the point clear — the structure of the missionary *congregation.* This would have forced the question: Is this a missionary congregation or something else?

Chapter 3: Evangelization

1. Historically, "evangelism" has been used in Anglo-American Protestant circles. We will use "evangelization" because it is translatable across linguistic and theological boundaries; it also conveys a less ideologically laden meaning.

2. P. T. Forsyth (1907:117). In the same vein, at a later point Forsyth wrote: "Christianity can endure, not by surrendering itself to the modern mind and modern culture, but rather by a break with it: the condition for a long future both for culture and the soul is the Christianity which antagonizes culture without denying its place. Culture asks but a half Gospel; and a half Gospel is no Gospel" (:131).

3. Alienation is an important theme in modern literature. See the two-volume compilation by Gerald Sykes (1964). For a critique of modern culture in the 1960s and 1970s, see Philip Slater (1976).

4. A recent work that models theological engagement with North American culture is Hall (1989).

5. See Roland Allen (1912); and (1960:89–113), "Mission Activities Considered in Relation to Manifestation of the Spirit."

6. Alfred C. Krass (1978 and 1982) has provided a model of *evangelistically* critical engagement with modern culture in two books. The latter draws on Krass's cross-cultural experience in West Africa and demonstrates the fresh leverage this gives for engagement with one's own culture.

Chapter 4: Church

1. Personal correspondence, W. R. Shenk to W. A. Visser 't Hooft, 5/11/81; WAV to WRS, 5/22/81.

2. Noting the silence of the New Testament Gospels on the founding of the church, Barth (1962:683f) concludes that the whole of the Gospel accounts are descriptions of the formation of this people of God.

3. One approach has been to establish the relationship between covenant community in the Old Testament and the church in the New through a careful study of terms as is done by Joseph E. Coleson, in Melvin E. Dieter and Daniel N. Berg, eds. (1984:3–25). This

leads to understatement of the archetypal power of the Abrahamic covenant.

4. In addition to Genesis 12:1–3, the Abrahamic covenant is found in 18:18, 22:18, 26:4, and 28:14. It has been suggested that this is the Old Testament form of the Great Commission.

5. The entire passage is an extended comment on the essentiality of mission to Christian existence.

6. Robert P. Wilder (1936:48) quotes *in extenso* reflections of Nettie Dunn Clark who wrote: "One reason for the great impression created by the Movement was that it made a clear, definite appeal for one cause only, and...a great mistake would be made if [it] were now to be made to cover both foreign and home missions, or the enlistment of young people for anything other than definite missionary work." This is a purely pragmatic and tactical argument but one that has long held sway. Samuel Zwemer (1943) based his interpretation of the Great Commission firmly on this dichotomy.

7. The genius of Christian faith is that it is not tied to a particular geography — holy city, holy land, holy language. Then comes the recurrent quest for total conquest of a particular country or people for Christ? Both Old and New Testaments are based on the conviction that the faith is preserved and transmitted through God's faithful remnant, a theme ignored in contemporary theology. Crusades and conquests comport well with Christendom but not with the biblical tradition.

8. It is not our purpose here to evaluate the modern mission movement. Recent studies that examine the reflex action of the modern mission movement on the Western church include A. F. Walls (1988:141–55) and W. R. Shenk (1984b:158–77; 1992:62–78).

9. Arias and Johnson (1992) demonstrate the importance of the Great Commission for full realization of the mission of the church. I want to press the point further: this can be achieved only by reconceptualizing the nature of the church in terms of the Great Commission.

10. This was a viewpoint that was important in the missiology of Gustav Warneck, from whose pioneering work (forged during the High Imperial period) much of modern missiology descends.

11. Sacerdotalism is irreconcilable with the prophetic office. Al-

though one must maintain the distinction between the apostolic and prophetic vocations, neither fits easily with the role of the priest whose role is to modulate conflict between church and society.

12. Modern commentators help to perpetuate a "Christendom" reading of the Acts account by the way they divide up the material and insert editorial heads and commentary that draw on modern practice and assumptions. Taking a random selection of commentaries, one notes that the majority introduce the term "mission" only at 9:32, with the beginning of the Gentile mission, or at 13:1–3: William Barclay (1953); F. F. Bruce (1954); I. Howard Marshall (1980). In contrast, Johannes Munck (1967) entitles 1:6–14, "The Mission to the World and the Ascension."

13. This does not mean all cultures are of the same moral caliber. Cultures may be deeply influenced by values that move them closer to the kingdom of God ideal. But at their best, such cultures remain marred by human fallibility.

14. This is not the place to pursue this important point. Rollo May (1969) has argued that the rise of psychiatric science is a direct response to modern culture but criticizes psychotherapy for being itself a part of the problem. See further, Menninger (1978).

15. One might start with an examination of the classical evangelical expression of conversion: "I have decided to accept Jesus as *my personal savior*." Revivalist culture arose concurrently with the Enlightenment and in its preoccupation with the self bears its imprint. Preoccupation with "self" turns religion into the instrument of self-fulfillment, a view difficult to reconcile with the call of Jesus to discipleship.

16. One area of modern culture where the role of violence is rising steadily is sports. On the one hand, sports dominate our culture to an extent frequently not acknowledged. On the other, it is becoming clear that exploitation and violence are essential to the sports system. The relation of sport and religion deserves close scrutiny, as reported by sports writer Frank Deford (1976) and more recently Shirl J. Hoffman (1992).

17. Karl Rahner (1991:124). For a more comprehensive treatment by Rahner, see (1983). Part 3 treats five themes descriptive of the kind of church he foresees: open, ecumenical, church from the roots,

democratized, sociocritical. It is significant that other leading theologians have emphasized these same themes. See Jürgen Moltmann (1977:7–11, 314–36); George A. Lindbeck (1971:226–43).

18. We distinguish here between renewal and ebbs and flows in church membership. Membership is hardly a reliable indicator of the health of the church. For example, the gains in United States church membership in the 1950s can be correlated with the economic prosperity of the period. Studies of that decade do not show this to have been a time of spiritual and theological renewal.

References Cited

Abraham, William J. 1989. *The Logic of Evangelism.* Grand Rapids: Eerdmans.

Allen, Roland. 1960. *The Ministry of the Spirit.* Grand Rapids: Eerdmans.

———. 1962. *Missionary Methods: St. Paul's or Ours?* Grand Rapids: Eerdmans. First published 1912.

Arias, Mortimer, and Alan Johnson. 1992. *The Great Commission: Biblical Models for Evangelism.* Nashville: Abingdon Press.

Barclay, William. 1953. *The Acts of the Apostles.* Philadelphia: Westminster Press.

Bardy, Gustave. 1988. Foreword. *Menschen werden Christen: Das Drama der Bekehrung in den ersten Jahrhunderten.* Freiburg im Breisgau: Herder.

Baritz, Loren. 1985. *Backfire: Vietnam — The Myths That Made Us Fight, The Illusions That Helped Us Lose, The Legacy That Haunts Us Today.* New York: Ballantine Books.

Barth, Karl. 1962. *Church Dogmatics: The Doctrine of Reconciliation.* Edinburgh: T & T Clark.

———. 1972. *The Epistle to the Romans.* Trans. Edwyn C. Hoskyns. London: Oxford University Press. First published 1933.

Barth, Karl, and Johannes Hamil. 1959. *How to Serve God in a Marxist Land.* New York: Association Press.

Barth, Markus. 1974. *Ephesians. The Anchor Bible.* Garden City: Doubleday and Co.

Bellah, Robert N., et al. 1986. *Habits of the Heart: Individualism and Commitment in American Life.* San Francisco: Harper & Row.

———. 1991. *The Good Society.* New York: A. A. Knopf.

Berger, Peter L. 1979. *Facing Up to Modernity.* Harmondsworth, Eng.: Penguin Books.

Berger, Peter, Brigitte Berger, and Hansfried Kellner. 1973. *The Homeless Mind: Modernization and Consciousness.* New York: Vintage Books.

Berkhof, Hendrikus. 1964. *The Doctrine of the Holy Spirit.* Richmond: John Knox Press.

————. 1979. *Christian Faith.* Grand Rapids: Eerdmans.

Bibby, Reginald W. 1987. *Fragmented Gods.* Toronto: Irwin Publishing.

Boff, Leonardo. 1986. *Ecclesiogenesis: The Base Communities Reinvent the Church.* Maryknoll: Orbis Books.

Bosch, David J. 1972. Systematic Theology and Missions: The Voice of an Early Pioneer. *Theologia Evangelica* 5:3:165–89.

————. 1982. Theological Education in Missionary Perspective, *Missiology* 10:1 (Jan.):13–34.

————. 1983. The Structure of Mission: An Exposition of Matthew 28:16–20, in *Exploring Church Growth,* W. R. Shenk, ed. (1983). Pp. 218–48.

————. 1991. *Transforming Mission: Paradigm Shifts in Theology of Mission.* Maryknoll: Orbis Books.

Brown, Colin. 1968. *Philosophy and the Christian Faith.* Downers Grove, Ill.: InterVarsity.

Bruce, F. F. 1954. *The Book of Acts.* Grand Rapids: Eerdmans.

Bruce, Steve, ed. 1992. *Religion and Modernization: Sociologists and Historians Debate the Secularization Thesis.* Oxford: Clarendon Press.

Brunner, Emil. 1931. *The Word and the World.* London: SCM Press.

Buber, Martin. 1950. *Two Types of Faith.* London: Routledge & Kegan Paul. Bungener, Pierre. 1959. The Worker-Priests: A French Protestant View. *Christianity and Crisis* 19:21 (Dec. 14): 180–84.

Busch, Eberhard, ed. 1976. *Karl Barth: His Life from Letters and Autobiographical Texts.* Philadelphia: Fortress Press.

Butterfield, Herbert. 1949. *Christianity and History.* London: G. Bell & Sons.

Church, F. Forrester, and Timothy George, eds. 1979. *Continuity and Discontinuity in Church History.* Leiden: E. J. Brill.

Coleson, Joseph E. 1984. Covenant Community in the Old Testament, in M. E. Dieter and D. N. Berg, eds. Pp. 3–25.

Colin, P., ed. 1989. *Les Catholiques Français et l'Héritage de 1789 — d'un centenaire à l'autre.* Paris: Beauchesne.

Collinson, Patrick. 1967. *The Elizabethan Puritan Movement.* London: Jonathan Cape.

Costas, Orlando E. 1989. *Liberating News: A Theology of Contextual Evangelization.* Grand Rapids: Eerdmans.

Cox, Harvey. 1965. *The Secular City: Secularization and Urbanization in Theological Perspective.* London: SCM Press.

———. 1984. *Religion in the Secular City.* New York: Simon & Schuster.

Davies, W. D., and D. C. Allison. 1992. Matt. 28:16–20: Texts Behind the Text. *Revue d'Histoire et de Philosophie Religieuses* 72:1:89–98.

Deford, Frank. 1976. Religion in Sport. *Sports Illustrated.* April 19, 26, and May 3.

Delumeau, Jean. 1977. *Catholicism Between Luther and Voltaire.* Philadelphia: Westminster Press.

Dieter, Melvin E., and Daniel N. Berg, eds. 1984. *An Inquiry into the Church.* Anderson: Warner Press.

Donovan, Leo J., S.J., ed. 1977. A Changing Ecclesiology in a Changing Church: A Symposium on Development in the Ecclesiology of Karl Rahner. *Theological Studies* 38:2 (Dec.): 736–62.

Driver, John. 1979. Mission — From a Believers' Church Perspective, *Mission Focus* 7:1 (March):1–6.

Dulles, Avery, S.J. 1989. A Half Century of Ecclesiology, *Theological Studies* 50:1 (Sept.):419–42.

Durnbaugh, Donald F. 1968. *The Believers' Church: The History and Character of Radical Protestantism.* New York: Macmillan.

Ellul, Jacques. 1967. *The Technological Society.* New York: Vintage Books. French orig. 1954.

Forsyth, P. T. 1907. *Positive Preaching and the Positive Mind.* New York: Eaton and Mains.

George, Carol V. R. 1993. *God's Salesman: Norman Vincent Peale and the Power of Positive Thinking.* New York: Oxford University Press.

Gilbert, Alan D. 1976. *Religion and Society in Industrial England.* London: Longman.

Green, Bryan. 1951. *The Practice of Evangelism.* New York: Charles Scribner's Sons.

Guinness, Os. 1993. *Dining with the Devil: The Megachurch Movement Flirts with Modernity.* Grand Rapids: Baker Book House.

Gunton, Colin. 1985. *Enlightenment and Alienation.* Grand Rapids: Eerdmans.

Hall, Douglas John. 1989. *Thinking the Faith: Christian Theology in the North American Context.* Minneapolis: Fortress Press.

Hammond, Phillip E., ed. 1985. *The Sacred in a Secular Age.* Berkeley: University of California Press.

Hardman, Keith J. 1990. *Charles Grandison Finney: Revivalist and Reformer.* Grand Rapids: Baker Book House. First published 1987.

Hastings, Adrian. 1986. *A History of English Christianity, 1920–1985.* London: Collins.

Hobhouse, Walter. 1911. *The Church and the World in Idea and History.* London: Macmillan. 2d ed.

Hoekendijk, J. C., and H. Schmidt. 1966. Morphological Fundamentalism, in Thomas Wieser, ed. Pp. 134–37.

Hoffman, Shirl J., ed. 1992. *Sport and Religion.* Champaign: Human Kinetics Books.

Hoge, Dean R. 1979. A Test of Theories of Denominational Growth and Decline, in Dean R. Hoge and David A. Roozen, eds. Pp. 179–97.

Hoge, Dean R., and David A. Roozen, eds. *Understanding Church Growth and Decline, 1950–1978.* Philadelphia: Pilgrim Press.

Hutchison, William R. 1982. *The Modernist Impulse in American Protestantism.* New York: Oxford University Press. Repr. 1976 ed.

John Paul II. 1990. On the Permanent Validity of the Church's Missionary Mandate. *Redemptoris Missio.* Washington: United States Catholic Conference.

Johnston, James, ed. 1888. *Report of the Missionary Conference on Protestant Missions of the World.* London: James Nisbet & Co.

Käsemann, Ernst. 1964. *Essays on New Testament Themes.* London: SCM Press.

Kelley, Dean M. 1972. *Why Conservative Churches Are Growing.* New York: Harper & Row.

Kenneson, Philip D. 1993. Selling [Out] the Church in the Marketplace of Desire. *Modern Theology* 9:4 (Oct.):319–48.

Kierkegaard, Søren. 1968. *Attack Upon "Christendom."* Trans. Walter Lowrie. Princeton: Princeton University Press. First published 1968.

Kraemer, Hendrik. 1958. *A Theology of the Laity.* Philadelphia: Westminster Press.

Krass, Alfred C. 1978. *Five Lanterns at Sundown: Evangelism in a Chastened Mood.* Grand Rapids: Eerdmans.

———. 1982. *Evangelizing Neopagan North America.* Scottdale: Herald Press.

Küng, Hans. 1967. *The Church.* New York: Sheed & Ward.

Lasch, Christopher. 1979. *The Culture of Narcissism.* New York: W. W. Norton & Co.

Legrand, Lucien. 1986. The Missionary Command of the Risen Christ. *Indian Theological Review* 23:3 (Sept.):290–309.

Lehmann, Helmut T., gen. ed., and U. S. Leupold, ed. 1965. *Luther's Works.* Philadelphia: Fortress Press.

Lewis, C. S. 1958. Rejoinder to Dr. Pittenger. *The Christian Century* 75:48 (Nov. 26):1359–61.

Lindbeck, George A. 1971. The Sectarian Future of the Church, in J. P. Whelan, S.J., ed. Pp. 226–43.

Littell, Franklin H. 1979. The Periodization of History, in F. F. Church and T. George, eds. Pp. 18–30.

Marsden, George M. 1980. *Fundamentalism and American Culture.* New York: Oxford University Press.

Marsden, George M., and Bradley J. Longfield, eds. 1992. *The Secularization of the Academy.* New York: Oxford University Press.

Marshall, I. Howard. 1980. *The Acts of the Apostles.* Grand Rapids: Eerdmans.

May, Rollo. 1969. *Love and Will.* New York: Norton.

McIlhaney, David B. 1988. *A Gentleman in Every Slum: Church of England Missions in East London, 1837–1914.* Allison Park, Pa.: Pickwick Publications.

McLeod, Hugh. 1980. The Dechristianization of the Working Class in Western Europe (1850–1900). *Social Compass* 27:2–3:191–214.

————. 1981. *Religion and the People of Western Europe, 1789–1970.* London: Oxford University Press.

Menninger, Karl. 1978. *Whatever Became of Sin?* New York: Hawthorne/Bantam. First published in 1973.

Michel, Otto. 1983. The Conclusion of Matthew's Gospel: A Contribution to the History of the Easter Message, in Graham Stanton, ed. Pp. 30–41. German orig. 1950.

Míguez Bonino, José. 1975. *Doing Theology in a Revolutionary Situation.* Philadelphia: Fortress Press.

Miller, Perry. 1966. *The Life of the Mind in America.* New York: Harcourt, Brace & World.

Moltmann, Jürgen. 1977. *The Church in the Power of the Spirit.* New York: Harper & Row.

Munck, Johannes. 1967. *The Acts of the Apostles. Anchor Bible.* Garden City: Doubleday & Co.

Myklebust, Olav G. 1957. *The Study of Missions in Theological Education.* 2 vols. Oslo: Egede Instituttet. First published 1955.

Neill, Stephen C. 1957. *The Unfinished Task.* London: Edinburgh House Press.

————. 1966. *The Church and Christian Union.* London: Oxford University Press.

Niebuhr, H. Richard, Wilhelm Pauck, and Francis P. Miller. 1935. *The Church Against the World.* Chicago/New York: Willet, Clark & Co.

Orme, William. 1828. *Memoir, Including Letters and Select Remains of John Urquhart.* Boston: Crocker & Brewster.

Outler, Albert. 1991. *John Wesley's Sermons: An Introduction.* Nashville: Abingdon Press. First published 1984.

Paton, David M. 1953. *Christian Missions and the Judgment of God.* London: SCM Press.

Pfeiffer, Edward. 1908. *Mission Studies.* Columbus: Lutheran Book Concern.

Pickard, Stephen K. 1993. Evangelism and the Character of Christian Theology. *Missionalia* 21:2 (Aug.):159–75.

Pope, Stephen. 1993. Expressive Individualism and True Self-Love: A Thomistic Perspective. *Journal of Religion* 71:3 (July):384–99.

Rahner, Karl. 1967. *The Christian of the Future.* New York: Herder & Herder.

———. 1983. *The Shape of the Church to Come.* New York: Crossroad. First published 1974.

———. 1991. *Theological Investigations.* Vol. XXII. *Human Society and the Church of Tomorrow.* New York: Crossroad.

Renard, Pierre. 1986. Cardinal Suhard and the New Evangelization. *Lumen Vitae* 41:3:350–54.

Romein, Jan. 1978. *The Watershed of Two Eras — Europe in 1900.* Trans. Arnold J. Pomerans. Middletown, Conn.: Wesleyan University Press.

Roof, Wade Clark, et al. 1979. Factors Producing Growth or Decline in United Presbyterian Congregations, in Dean R. Hoge and David A. Roozen, eds.

Rosell, Garth M. 1984. Charles G. Finney: His Place in the Stream of American Protestantism, in L. I. Sweet, ed.

Rudnick, Milton L. 1984. *Speaking the Gospel Through the Ages: A History of Evangelism.* St. Louis: Concordia Publishing House.

Sandeen, Ernest R. 1978 repr. *The Roots of Fundamentalism.* Grand Rapids: Baker Book House.

Schnackenburg, Rudolf. 1965. *The Church in the New Testament.* New York: Herder & Herder.

Shaull, Richard. 1991. *The Reformation and Liberation Theology.* Louisville: Westminster/John Knox.

Shelley, Bruce, and Marshall Shelley. 1992. *Consumer Church.* Downers Grove, Ill.: InterVarsity.

Shenk, Wilbert R. 1983. *Exploring Church Growth.* Grand Rapids: Eerdmans.

———, ed. 1984a. *Anabaptism and Mission.* Scottdale: Herald Press.

———. 1984b. The "Great Century" Reconsidered, in W. R. Shenk, ed. 1984a. Pp. 158–77.

————. 1992. Reflections on the Modern Missionary Movement: 1792–1992. *Mission Studies* 9:1 (17):62–78.

Slater, Philip. 1976. *The Pursuit of Loneliness: American Culture at the Breaking Point.* Boston: Beacon Press.

Solzhenitsyn, Aleksandr I. 1972. *The Nobel Lecture on Literature.* New York: Harper & Row.

Stacey, John, ed. 1988. *John Wesley: Contemporary Perspectives.* London: Epworth Press.

Stanton, Graham, ed. 1983. *Interpretation of Matthew.* Philadelphia: Fortress Press.

Sugden, E. H., ed. 1921. *The Standard Sermons of John Wesley.* London: Epworth Press.

Suhard, Emmanuel. 1953. *The Church Today: The Collected Writings of Emmanuel Cardinal Suhard.* Chicago: Fides Publishers.

Sweet, Leonard I., ed. 1984. *The Evangelical Tradition in America.* Macon: Mercer University Press.

Sykes, Gerald, ed. 1964. *Alienation: The Cultural Climate of Our Time.* 2 vols. New York: George Braziller.

Tavard, George H. 1992. *The Church, Community of Salvation.* Collegeville, Minn.: Michael Glazier/Liturgical Press.

Thompson, E. P. 1966. *The Making of the English Working Class.* New York: Vintage Books.

————. 1971. The Moral Economy of the English Crowd in the Eighteenth Century. *Past and Present* 50 (Feb.):76–136.

Towards the Conversion of England. 1945. London: The Press and Publications Board of the Church Assembly.

Van Engen, Charles E. 1992. *God's Missionary People: Rethinking the Purpose of the Local Church.* Grand Rapids: Baker Book House.

Vidal, Maurice. 1989. Initiatives ecclesiales du Cardinal Suhard, in P. Colin, ed. Pp. 225–37.

Visser 't Hooft, W. A. 1974. Evangelism in the Neo-Pagan Situation. *International Review of Mission* 73:249 (Jan.):81–86.

————. 1977. Evangelism among Europe's Neo-Pagans. *International Review of Mission* 66:264 (Oct.):349–60.

Walls, A. F. 1988. Missionary Societies and the Fortunate Subversion of the Church. *The Evangelical Quarterly* 60:2:141–55.